*To Brian,
Keep the If.,*
Craig Colby

ALL CAPS

STORIES THAT JUSTIFY AN OUTRAGEOUS HAT COLLECTION

BY CRAIG COLBY

One Printers Way
Altona, MB R0G 0B0
Canada

www.friesenpress.com

Copyright © 2022 by Craig Colby
First Edition — 2022

You can find out more about Craig Colby and his work at www.colbyvision.net

All rights reserved.

No part of this publication may be reproduced in any form, or by any means, electronic or mechanical, including photocopying, recording, or any information browsing, storage, or retrieval system, without permission in writing from FriesenPress.

This book is not sponsored by, affiliated with, or endorsed by any of the brands presented within.

Cover photo by Mark Foerster, CSC
Portrait photo by Veronica Kucherova, Vongue Art Photography
All hat photos by Craig Colby

ISBN
978-1-03-914879-6 (Hardcover)
978-1-03-914878-9 (Paperback)
978-1-03-914880-2 (eBook)

1. BIOGRAPHY & AUTOBIOGRAPHY, SPORTS

Distributed to the trade by The Ingram Book Company

Readers' Comments

"ALL CAPS had me identifying with so many of my own experiences. It had me laughing and shedding a tear."

Rod Smith,
TSN Sportscaster

"As a long time strapback fan, I love Craig Colby's heartfelt tribute to his beloved ball caps."

Lisa Bowes, Sportscaster and Author
of the Best-Selling "Lucy Tries Sports" series.

"A witty, sentimental, heartbreaking, joyous journey where family, life and sports collide. This is masterful storytelling at its finest."

Teresa Kruze – Broadcaster
and Best-selling Author

This book is dedicated to
my mother, Dorothy, a teacher and writer,
and my father, Peter, a scientist and painter.

Thank you for showing me
that creativity is part of life.

Guide for Non-Hat Fanatics

Structured—This hat has a stiff form underneath the front dome, giving the hat some architecture.

Unstructured—This hat does not have any rigid substructure. It's a floppy cloth cap that hugs your head.

Fullback—This type of hat is cloth all the way around. There are no adjustable straps. It can come in sizes from extra-large to small, but is more likely one of the next two types.

Fitted—This hat has a specific size that matches your head. My hat size is 7⅜ or 7 ¼.

Flexfit—This hat has a full cloth back but stretches to fit your head.

Strapback—A band of cloth in the back of the hat is adjusted to fit your head.

Velcro Strapback—The band in the back of the hat is secured with Velcro.

Snapback—The hat size is adjusted by a series of plastic snaps in the back of the hat.

You'll find QR codes throughout the book. Scan them with the camera on your phone or tablet for bonus content.

Introduction

This book isn't about hats. Sure, there are a lot of hats in it. You'll read about why some are great, and others are terrible. I'll also talk about logos, uniforms, stadiums, and teams. However, the book could just as easily feature pictures from a collection of shoes or stamps and the heart of it would be the same.

This book is about what the hats mean—connections.

In the middle of March 2020, a week into the great COVID-19 pandemic lockdown, I decided to wear a different hat every day until people could be together again. Just for fun, I posted the day's hat on Facebook. I didn't realize three things at the time: how long we'd be locked down, how many hats I had, or how people would respond.

I started adding little stories about each day's hat—where I got it, who I was with, and what each hat meant to me. People started sharing their own hats and stories. When someone ran out of caps, they'd offer up pictures, autographs, or bobbleheads, just to stay in the conversation. As loneliness engulfed us, this was a way to come together.

After 125 days, I ran out of hats. I thought that would be it. Nope. People told me they were sad it was over, and not just the show-and-tellers. Lurkers chimed in about how much they'd enjoyed the posts. My wife's cousin Deb said it had replaced the horoscope as her morning read. A week later, I started sharing shirts, and Deb got in on that.

We all long for connection. The COVID-19 Hat Marathon linked me to those who participated, and to my own history. Each day, I wore a different part of my life. That felt great during a time when I often felt uneasy.

Here is my hat collection, not as it appeared in the pandemic posts, but reorganized with my newfound appreciation for the tale the caps tell. So, welcome to my connections. This book is filled with stories that have brought me to my knees in both laughter and tears. If that interests you, this book is for you.

If you just like hats, there are a lot of those, too.

Detroit Tigers Home Cap
Style: solid plastic,
adjustable snap inside
Purchased in the late 2000s at Comerica Park,
Detroit, Michigan.

The first hat I remember owning was a plastic Detroit Tigers helmet just like this one.

In the mid-to-late 1960s, I lived in Ann Arbor, Michigan, a university town, with my parents, Peter and Dorothy, and my brothers, Jim, three years older, and Scott, two years younger. We lived in a white two-story house on Lakewood Drive, with a big backyard and a friendly cherry tree just begging to be climbed. Our home was around the corner and down the street from school. Every day, I insisted on walking to school by myself.

If you turned the other way at the end of our driveway, you'd arrive at a lake, where my brothers and I would search for frogs. My childhood was a comforting pocket of comic books, bike rides with friends, and watching "The Little Rascals" on the black-and-white television in our sunroom while sitting in my dad's lap.

Surrounding that pocket was social upheaval. Even at four years old, I was aware that Detroit, just forty-five minutes east, was burning during the race riots of 1967. News of the civil rights movement was ubiquitous. Students from Black neighborhoods were bused into schools in white neighborhoods across the US, including our own. That's how I met two of my best friends, Charlie and Cyril.

When I asked if Charlie could come over to play, Mom had to call Charlie's mom and we had to drive across town to pick him up. I only recall it happening once. I do recall my Grade 2 teacher smiling down at Cyril, who looked concerned, and telling him: "Say it loud: I'm Black and I'm proud." It didn't occur to me that Cyril and Charlie felt different in class. Soon, I would get a taste of that myself.

In 1968, another event in Detroit dominated our world: The Detroit Tigers beat the St. Louis Cardinals to win the World Series. I was too young to follow anything but the excitement. Still, the names of those players were heard as frequently as those of my classmates.

Bill Freehan, Mickey Lolich, Denny McLain, Willie Horton, and, of course, Al Kaline were legendary figures, as heroic to us kids as Spider-Man. The Tigers were more than just a baseball team: They were a unifying force in a turbulent time. The 1968 Tigers gave everyone something to feel good about. To me, they were symbols of happiness from my childhood in Michigan, a time that was about to end.

In 1971, about a month before I turned eight, we moved to Canada. My dad, a fisheries research scientist, landed a job with Ontario's Ministry of Natural Resources, to lead the Walleye Research Unit. It was a big move, but it meant that my folks could buy a house.

I wasn't happy about it. It meant leaving everyone I'd ever known. I didn't even know where Canada was. Grandpa Dutch, Dad's father, attempted to reassure me.

"It will be fine," he said. "They have this great sport up there called hockey. The players beat the hell out of each other all the time." It wasn't much of an incentive.

The move was exactly as traumatic as I was afraid it would be. We left Ann Arbor right after one of my brother Jim's baseball games. He was still in his uniform and his teammates were crying as our station wagon pulled away.

It took two days to arrive at our new home in Thunder Bay, Ontario, on the north shore of Lake Superior, a blue-collar city built around the pulp and paper industry with grain elevators servicing ships in the harbor.

The locals didn't roll out the welcome mat.

We arrived at the end of the school year, and I could see children walking down the hill behind our house from the school we would attend in the fall. One day, in an attempt to make friends, I jumped out at them in my Spider-Man costume. Someone beat me up. The Vietnam war dominated the news and Americans were unpopular in Canada anyway. Kids threw rocks at our house and yelled, "Yankee go home!" When I talked, children made fun of my accent.

We looked like all the other white kids in the neighborhood, but our new peers made sure we knew that we were different. The message was clear: "You don't belong here." It was even worse for my Indigenous schoolmates. Two brothers in my class were regularly bullied while they walked home through the forested hill behind the school. One day, in self-defense, one of the brothers pulled out a knife and used it. He was sent off to a school for juvenile delinquents.

No, I didn't belong in Thunder Bay, and I wasn't sure I wanted to. When we were called into the staff room to watch Team Canada play Team Russia in the legendary 1972 Summit Series, I was the only one not on the edge of my seat desperate for Canada to win a hockey game. Like a lot of immigrants, I held onto things that made me feel close to home

As an adult, I saw this hat at the Tigers' home stadium, Comerica Park. I bought it immediately, and brought it home for my two sons, Shane and Curtis. They never wore it, not even once. The band that adjusts the size poked the back of their heads. Really, it's not a very good hat. For them, it lacked the one thing it had in abundance for me: warm feelings of my idyllic childhood in Michigan, memories of running around, playing with my brothers and friends, and waiting to hear if Jim finally got an Al Kaline baseball card at the gas station down the street. The best hats are more than shaped cloth. They're links to the happiest parts of our lives and the people who created them.

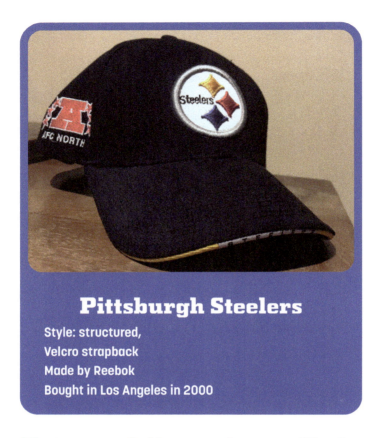

Pittsburgh Steelers

Style: structured,
Velcro strapback
Made by Reebok
Bought in Los Angeles in 2000

Jim and Scott were good athletes, crazy about sports. When I was young, I was neither. I was so convinced that I was hopelessly uncoordinated that I avoided sports completely. Comic books were my refuge.

Still, when friends wanted to play pick-up football, I did. I played well enough that I decided to try out for the football team in high school. I was nervous as hell. In Grade 9, at the first team meeting, a guy I knew from public school, one year older, walked into the room and glared at me. "You're playing? I quit!" I stayed for the meeting but didn't come back for tryouts. I ran cross country for Hillcrest High School instead, but it didn't inspire any passion in me.

In Grade 10, I tried again, expecting to be cut. Not only did I make the team, but I started at offensive guard. I was stunned. Although I was grateful, I longed to play defense because I loved tackling. When my testosterone kicked in during puberty, I found knocking someone on their ass very satisfying. All season, I campaigned to play on the other side of the ball. For the last game, they put me in at defensive end. I dropped the opponent's running back behind the line of scrimmage on the first series. After two series, the opponents started double-teaming me. For the first time, I felt like an athlete.

Even though our team went 0-7, I loved playing football. I started watching the NFL. Most sports allegiances are determined by geography—you cheer for whichever team is closest. Thunder Bay was remote enough to be no man's land. We lived close enough to Minnesota that the Vikings were the most popular option, but it wasn't a requirement.

Out of loyalty to Michigan, I cheered for the Detroit Lions, but they were so bad we never saw them on TV. Not so for the Pittsburgh Steelers. They were mean on defense and their black jerseys with gold trim and gold pants with a thick black stripe were gorgeous. The combination was tough with just enough "look at me" flair. Having the logo on just one side of their helmets gave them a little swagger, too. The Steelers became my team.

I didn't know anyone else who cheered for Pittsburgh, so my choice didn't bring a group of like-minded friends with it. But I was associating myself with the Steelers identity. It gave me a little boost in confidence, even if no one else saw me as a symbol of swaggering toughness. When we were talking about football, my peers would say, "Craig's a Steelers fan." I liked that calling card.

My football-loving family welcomed me to the shared passion. For Christmas, Mom and Dad gave me a Steelers hat and shirt. A month later, when the Steelers beat the Cowboys to win the Super Bowl, I was hooked.

This is not the hat my parents gave me. That hat was terrible, with a plastic mesh back with a plastic front and a shapeless brim. I wore it constantly. This hat replaced my first, many years later.

My last three years of football, I played linebacker. I was even named a team captain, an honor beyond my expectations. One play encapsulates my high school football experience. In my senior year, we were playing

Lakeview High School. Both our teams were winless. Every time they punted, a guy I'd played touch football with, we called him OJ, would block me as I rushed the punter.

OJ was fast and strong, but he bailed out early every time. I told my teammates, "I'm getting one of those punts." Sure enough, in the third quarter, I blew past OJ and arrived just as the punter was about to kick the ball. I launched into the path of the ball. It hit me in the forearms and ricocheted behind the punter.

When I landed, I saw about fifty yards of unoccupied field, our end zone, and the football uncharacteristically bouncing straight up and down. I went straight for the ball, caught it chest high, and tore off for the goal line. I couldn't feel anyone getting close. When I crossed into the end zone, I threw the ball in the air as high as I could, then turned to welcome my teammates, who jumped all over me. Then I saw the yellow flag, way back down the field.

My teammate George Bruley, a big, tough hockey player in his first and only year of football, saw someone passing him, but nowhere close to me, grabbed the opponent's shoulder for a moment, then let go. My dad told me the ref looked at the grab, hesitated, then threw the flag. Even though it didn't have any effect on the play, George had committed a penalty. The ball would come back to the spot of the infraction. The only touchdown I would ever score was called back. We lost that game 13-7.

The deck was always stacked against Hillcrest. Half our student body bused in from the country and couldn't stay for practice. In my senior year, we had twenty-two players; you need twenty-four in Canadian football. We couldn't even scrimmage the defense against the offense. We had to run one side of the offense against one side of the defense. It's impossible to win like that, and a lot of the other students made fun of us. Still, I'm overly proud of having been a captain of the football team. I loved playing football and being identified as a football player. It gave me the confidence to try other things beyond football I never thought I'd be able to do.

Hillcrest High School

Style: structured snapback

Bought at Hillcrest in the early 1980s

In Grade 10, I shared a study class with Dave Hagberg. I'd met Dave in Grade 9. He was a hockey player and looked like it—athletic, with blond hair and eyes so blue they were almost white. He wore a jean jacket and shades every day. Dave didn't say much, which added to his cool aura. I was thin with big glasses and brown hair that I let grow way too long then had cut way too short. Because I made people laugh, I talked too much. There was nothing cool about me.

Dave and I bonded over a common adversary: our study room teacher Ms. Douglas, an attractive, blonde woman in her late twenties, who sported stylish clothes and an air of casual superiority. She barely looked at us and certainly didn't want to hear us. If we did or said anything in the class, we were sent to the office. Dave or I was there every other day.

Finding the bottom end of her tolerance became a game. We'd see how innocuous an act of defiance could be to still earn banishment. One day we turned her desk around before she arrived, so she couldn't put her legs underneath. Ms. Douglas looked around, and since there was no clear culprit, sat sideways without acknowledging the change. In one class, Dave put his shoe on his desk. Ms. Douglas told him to put it back on his foot. Dave refused. To the office with you! The next day when Ms. Douglas came into the room, the entire class had one shoe on their desk. She said nothing.

Eventually, the school vice-principal, Mr. Vukovich, told Dave that if we were sent to the office one more time, we'd be banished outside to clean up the garbage on the lawn. When Dave told me about the threat, I said "That's great! We can be outside instead of in here."

The next day, after about ten minutes of sitting quietly, Dave and I raised our hands in tandem, like a synchronized swimming routine. Ms. Douglas looked concerned. "What is it?"

"Can you please send us to the office?"

She looked more concerned. "Why?"

"We just think we should be there."

Ms. Douglas kept pressing us until we 'fessed up. Frankly, she looked relieved, both with the answer and that she'd be rid of us. We spent the spring outside. First, we'd clean up the garbage, then we'd watch the Grade 9 girls in gym class on the field across the street.

Dave and I became inseparable. In Grade 11, we started doing school announcements, little skits with characters and music. They were popular with the students and the staff. We both played football and helped run the school paper, which was just a platform for us to write funny stories. Funny to us, anyway

I was vice-president of the student council and played clarinet in the band. Dave played for the hockey team. I'd watch all of his games, often with his parents. Our hockey team won the city championship two years in a row.

The second year, student council president Shawn Untinen and I threw school hats, like the one shown here, into the stands during breaks in play, whipping up the fans. Shawn and I predated the T-shirt cannon. This is a terrible hat, uncomfortable and ugly. The front is foam, the back is plastic. It doesn't hold its shape. The logo is a patch that was sewn on. Still, I can't part with it.

I know high school is hard for a lot of people, but it was wonderful for me. When Dave and I graduated, Dave was the co-male student athlete of the year, and I was the valedictorian. I still didn't feel like I belonged in Canada, but I felt like I belonged on a football team, at school, and in my friendship with Dave.

Highway 61

Style: unstructured, strapback
Made by Bluescentric
A gift from my cousin Julie at the end of the COVID Hat Marathon

Dave and I were huge John Belushi and Dan Aykroyd fans. We loved the Blues Brothers, dressing up as them for Halloween. Dave was Elwood and I was Jake. When Belushi died on March 5, 1982—Dave's nineteenth birthday—we put together a Blues Brothers cover band for the school talent show. We'd both been in our high school production of "Guys and Dolls," so we'd been trained to sing enough to think we could pull it off.

The performance was listed as "a tribute to John Belushi." Our friend John Petrynka barked out our introduction over the full band rocking the refrain from Otis Redding's "I Can't Turn You Loose," and we walked in from the back of the auditorium. Girls screamed! It was intoxicating. We played our two songs and left to thunderous applause. The performance went so well, we entered the citywide Tommy Horricks' Talent Show, held in local bars.

Our teenage band of wannabe bluesmen and women sauntered into the Hodder Tavern after dark on a school night. Only Dave was old enough to be there. The room was filled with family, friends, and drunk cowboys and bikers. While we waited backstage to make our entrance, one biker threatened Dave and me and propositioned my mom. We were a long way from the friendly home field of the high school auditorium. We had no idea how we would be received.

The band took the stage first and John delivered the introduction: "Gooooood EEEEvening, ladies and gentlemen, and welcome to the Hodder!" Dave and I strolled out from the back room, hopped up on stage, and opened the closest thing we had to a briefcase full of blues: a huge brown metallic typewriter case. Dave took out a harmonica, then we hit our pose as the song punctuated its final note.

The lights were bright, and since I was wearing sunglasses, I could only see about five feet in front of me. But I heard applause. We immediately went into "Everybody Needs Somebody (to Love)." When it ended, the bar exploded with cheers. We played "Soul Man," then went backstage, doing our best to remain expressionlessly in character, despite the flush of triumph swelling inside us. Two euphoric cowboys rushed in, shook our hands, and said, "Take this show on the road!"

We won the competition that night, qualifying for the city finals at the Canadian Lakehead Exhibition. There was a small midway with a few pedestrian rides, food stands, and a mainstage where the big acts played. That's where we performed.

We did our act once in the afternoon and again for the finals at night. Dave and I stood in the crowd nonchalantly. When the introduction music played, we rushed to the stage, opened the briefcase, and retrieved the harmonica. Then I did a cartwheel and we hit our pose. The crowd was sparse but filled with friends and family. We had a great time.

After the evening show, they announced the winner of the citywide competition. A talented local singer won first prize: the opportunity to make a record. We were given gift certificates for a steakhouse.

The Blues Brothers were my gateway drug to the blues. I started buying blues albums. The music became part of my life. But by far the best part of the band experience was being on stage with my best friend, fronting a band of close pals, doing something none of us would have thought possible on our own.

We continued to play shows at a rodeo and bars around town that summer. A promoter approached us about playing some dances—or boogies, as they were called in Thunder Bay—in the fall. Since I was going out of town to school, we had to decline.

The night before I left for university in Windsor, Ontario, we played another Tommy Horricks' Talent Show. We played four songs, then left for the night. We didn't care if we won, we just wanted to play one last time before I left Thunder Bay.

After the show, Dave drove me back to my house in his 1978 brown Camero Z-28. It was another symbol of his coolness—one he earned. Dave bought the car with cash he saved from landscaping work he'd done since he was fourteen.

When we pulled up to my house, I didn't know what I was going to say. Dave had become that one true friend you are lucky to find in a lifetime. I knew he felt the same way. We were closer than brothers. How do you encapsulate that in a couple of sentences?

Dave didn't even try. He gave me a big hug, a wordless gesture that said everything. Then he got in his car and drove away. We'd each be facing whatever adventures came next on our own.

This is my blues hat. The 61 stands for Highway 61, which follows the mighty Mississippi from Louisiana to Minnesota and crosses the border to end in Thunder Bay. Despite some renaming in places, the route is still there.

Starting In the early twentieth century and right through the Second World War, Black agricultural workers from the Deep South followed this route north to seek better jobs and better lives. This decades-long event became known as the Great Migration. These migrants brought the blues with them to big cities like Detroit and Chicago. Highway 61 is called the Blues Highway because so many musicians travelled the route. It's also where Robert Johnson allegedly made a deal with the devil to gain the skills to become a great bluesman.

A lot of people think the blues is just sad songs, but the songs are about the breadth of life, from "How Blue Can You Get" to "Let the Good Times Roll." The blues is about being genuine. Dave and I were always real with each other. We could, and would, talk about anything. We'd be in each other's corner, through good times and bad. Dave and I really were blues brothers.

This is my blues hat. If someone recognizes the significance of Highway 61 when they see this lid, I know they're cool. It's also a comfortable cotton hat that holds its shape well.

Detroit Tigers - Home
Style: structured, fitted
Made by New Era, 5950
Bought at Tiger Stadium in the late 1990s

In September 1982, I arrived in Windsor, Ontario, for my first year at university. I didn't know anyone, and the airline lost my luggage. Overnight, I went from popular to nobody. It was a difficult, but worthwhile, experience. Sometimes, you need everything that defines you to be taken away. Then you stop asking *what* you are and start asking *who* you are.

I walked onto the University of Windsor's compact campus—a mix of stately brick buildings straight out of a brochure and the charmless Brutalist-style blocks popular in the '60s and '70s.

I was enrolled in an honors B.A. in communications and English. Windsor was the only school that offered this combination. That's one reason I chose it. Another lay on the other side of the Detroit River, beckoning like a siren to this rabid Detroit sports fan.

What I lost in identity I gained in purpose. That purpose was to see a Tigers game. In my first month of school, my residence organized a bus trip to see the Tigers play the Red Sox. I bought a ticket and headed down the street to Nantais Sports to buy my first Tigers hat—the first of many. It had a foam front and a plastic mesh back with an adjustable strap. Even though it was poor quality, I loved having a Tigers hat. It's not the one pictured here.

On game day, September 19, 1982, I hopped on the bus. Since I didn't know anyone on the tour, I sat by myself. It was better that way. I figured everyone else was just going to a ball game. I was on a quest to sacred ground. Tiger Stadium was a legend from my earliest childhood memories. This baseball mecca, which opened less than a week after the Titanic sank, had always seemed distant and unattainable—odd for a place that sells tickets to every game.

My heart was racing as our group entered the storied stadium at the corner of Michigan and Trumbull. It was like stepping into a time machine. I thought about the millions of Tigers fans who had sat right here watching our team. I thought about the generations of my family that cheered for the Tigers. Those connections flowed through me.

I walked through the concourse, and emerged on the upper deck, above third base. Tingles ran through my body. The brilliant afternoon sky was open above—robin's egg blue decorated with whisps of cloud. The field of play was vibrant, like a painting come to life below. Emerald grass was surrounded by navy blue seats, with a few rows of orange seats in the upper deck, extending all the way around the stadium.

We took our seats, about halfway to the top of the upper deck. Pillars supported the upper deck and roof, obstructing the view for some, but those supports put us right on top of the action. This was baseball heaven. The Tigers took the field in their home whites, the same uniforms they had worn since my parents were in diapers. I was so excited I was almost trembling.

That feeling lasted the entire game; it was a little like falling in love. My bond with the team, the fans, and my own family history, was thrilling. I was hooked, even though the Tigers lost to the Red Sox thanks to a Carney Lansford grand slam in the eighth. From that day, being a Tigers fan would be part of who I was.

It helped that the Tigers were a team on the rise. Two years later, they made it to the World Series, facing the San Diego Padres. I camped outside the stadium overnight to get tickets with my girlfriend Susan May. My buddy Dave Matthews (we all called him Dog) and his girlfriend joined us.

It was mid-September, so the days were temperate, but the nights were crisp. Susan and I brought a comforter and our textbooks and studied under the streetlights with our backs against the stadium. An ABC news crew interviewed us about our pilgrimage. We ate White Castle burgers for dinner and slept as well as we could on the cold concrete. It was a small price for what we hoped would be a glorious payoff. In the morning, when the ticket booth opened, we bought three obstructed-view seats to Game Four for Susan, my brother Scott, and me. The trip back to Windsor felt like victory.

We arrived on game day geared up. I wore a Tigers jacket, home jersey, and hat. Scott wore a home jersey. Susan wore a Tigers T-shirt under her winter coat. We sat underneath the press box behind home plate and watched the announcers arrive. We yelled to Vin Scully (who waved), Joe Garagiola (who posed theatrically with his arms out like a victorious gladiator), and Bob Costas (who ignored us but waved at a blonde woman in a tight white dress who called to him).

The obstruction was a pole in our line of sight between second and third base. That day Alan Trammell hit two two-run homers, solidifying him as my favorite player ever. Jack Morris pitched a complete game in a 4-2 victory. The Tigers took a 3-1 series lead.

The next day Scott, Susan, and I watched Game Five at a crowded Irish pub down the street from the stadium as the Tigers clinched their fourth World Series Championship. We ran into the street with other Tigers fans, high-fiving people in cars and hugging strangers in Tigers garb. Those were two of the best days of my life.

Before the World Series, I bought my first New Era 5950 home Tigers hat, size 7⅜. It was as distant from the other hats I'd owned as humans are from the small mammals that scurried through the undergrowth when the dinosaurs ruled the Earth.

A solid mesh on the inside gave the front dome a pristine shape. The brim was stiff, yet easy to curve. The Tigers' olde English D stitched in white glowed against the midnight blue background. What a thing of beauty. It was like wearing art and architecture. This was the first hat I ever loved.

An article in "USA Today" confirmed my heavily biased opinion that the Tigers hat is the best in baseball. It has all the elements of a classic Major League Baseball cap. The logo is a simple but stylish letter representing the home city. There are also very few colors. Two is perfect. Three works as well, but no more than that. All the great, historic MLB hats follow these simple guidelines for a classy look.

That first hat is long gone. I wore it until it shrank from sweat. The hat pictured here is probably my third or fourth Tigers home New Era 5950 hat. When one gets a little shabby, I buy a new one, but keep the old ones to wear when it's raining, or I'm going to be sweating. I only get rid of one when it's completely unwearable.

The Detroit Tigers New Era 5950 opened the door to my hat obsession.

Detroit Red Wings
Style: structured, fitted
Made by New Era, 5950
Purchased in the 2000s

When we moved to Canada, my parents decided we would ski, not play hockey. Winter weekends would be spent shushing down the slopes, not bundled in dank rinks. We didn't even watch hockey. When my dad, Pete, attended a Thunder Bay Twins game, the local semi-pro team, he was selected to take part in a giveaway at intermission. If he could shoot the puck into a slot in the net from center ice, he'd win a prize. Dad's friend John told the person sitting next to him, "Watch this guy. He was drafted by the NHL." Dad shot . . . and missed the net completely. His friend John fell over laughing. Dad defended his poor performance, saying, "It wasn't fair! The blade was curved!" In case you're not a hockey fan, it's supposed to be.

I started to follow hockey by watching Dave's high school games. Then, on Saturday nights, I watched the NHL with Dave and our friends John O'Gorman (JohnO), Rob Kapatan, Darrell Maunula, and Walter Flasza. I learned a lot, but I didn't have a team.

That changed when I went to university. As it had for the Tigers games, our residence arranged a trip to see the Detroit Red Wings play Wayne Gretzky's Edmonton Oilers. My seat was four rows from the ice. Being so close to the speed and artistry of the players was entrancing. The Great One had three assists in the Oilers victory. My eye was caught by another player though. John Ogrodnick had two goals and two assists for the Wings, becoming my first favorite player. I became a Red Wings fan that night.

They didn't make it easy though. In 1982-83, they were one of the worst teams in the league. When I went to the Wings home opener in 1983, the owner, Mike Ilitch, stood in the concourse and apologized for the team's poor play.

On January 20, 1984, I went to a game against the Minnesota North Stars. The Wings allowed four goals on the first eight shots on net. When the attendance was announced, people booed. The fans booed themselves for coming to the game. I'd never seen that before and I've never seen it since.

The team on the ice may have been terrible but their uniforms and logo were perfection. The red-and-white color scheme stood out on the ice, and a winged wheel is perfect iconography for a Detroit team, a nod to the speed of hockey and the Motor City's industrial identity. This is my favorite logo. Gorgeous!

Go Wings!

Detroit Lions

Style: structured, Velcro strapback
Made by Sports Specialties
Given to me by my brother Scott in the 2000s

The Lions Honolulu Blue and Silver merchandise is gorgeous, and the logo looks great. Hang on to those redeeming qualities. You'll need them.

The Lions are the bane of a Detroit sports fan. The last time they won the championship was 1957, just a few days after my parents got married. In my lifetime, they have just one playoff victory. But because my family is from Michigan, we love them.

In 1983, the Lions fielded a good team, even winning their division, so I saw them three times. One victory was over my beloved Steelers, 45-3 on American Thanksgiving, a mixed blessing for me.

In 1984, encouraged by the Lions upswing, my family came to Windsor over Canadian Thanksgiving so we could all see a Lions game together. What fun!

The Lions turned over the ball ten times on seven interceptions and three fumbles in a 28-7 loss to the Broncos. It was one of the worst performances in NFL history. Fans streamed out of the Silverdome in the fourth quarter. We stayed. Jim, Scott, and I moved into vacant seats behind the Lions bench.

My brothers and I sat in a tidal wave of unrestrained invective. A Lions lineman started yelling at the fans who were pelting him with wadded-up pieces of the game program. Gary Danielson, the Lions starting quarterback, who threw four of the interceptions, pulled the lineman away. The linemen complied but put his helmet on to protect himself from the debris. Who knew what the fans would throw next?

In the middle of this firestorm, Jim yelled out "Go Lions!"

And that's what it's like to be a Lions fan.

Detroit Tigers- Road
Style: structured, fitted
Made by New Era, 5950
Purchased in the 2000s

In high school, I was popular but not particularly attractive. Despite playing football, I was skinny, with huge glasses. I looked more like a clarinetist in the band, which I was, than a jock. My giant hair and the football jerseys I wore every day didn't help. The girl I dated was looking for someone better, clearly with good reason. I also suffered in comparison to my best friend, Dave, or my brother Scott, or before that, my brother Jim. Dave, Scott, and Jim were handsome and athletic. I was friendly and funny, so I had a few fans, but the consensus was "I'll take a pass."

That changed for me in 1983, my second year of university, when a pretty, strawberry-blonde social work student named Susan saw something in me. She was smart, fun at a party, and loved sports. We fell in love quickly, despite her habit of calling me "pookie bear." It was serious. I finally knew what it was like to connect with someone deeply, to have our lives intertwined. I passed on the extra-curriculars I'd loaded up on in high school to spend time with Susan. We were inseparable.

Unfortunately, we fought—a little at first, then a lot.

In the summer of 1986, Nordair (which shut down the next year) offered standby passes on any of their flights for a month. I flew down from Thunder Bay for my graduation from the University of Windsor. The next weekend, I travelled to see Susan in St. Catharines, an hour south of Toronto.

I arrived on Friday night. On Saturday, I wore a Detroit Tigers road hat when we went to see the Tigers play the Toronto Blue Jays in Exhibition Stadium. Susan and I bickered throughout the game. That was fine. The Tigers were leading 5-1 in the seventh, so all was right in the world. In the eighth, the Tigers gave up three runs. Now I was annoyed. In the ninth inning, Willie Hernandez, the Tigers' 1984 Cy Young Award winner and MVP, gave up a leadoff homer to Cliff Johnson, which tied the game.

The Blue Jay fans around us jumped and cheered. I glowered. Then the Jays' Buck Martinez jacked a walk-off home run for the win. My mood fell with the Tigers. Now every slight was magnified.

Susan and I fought the rest of the night, climaxing in a barroom "That's it" confrontation. I slept in my clothes so I could make a beeline for the door in the morning. Susan's father drove me to the airport for the first flight to Thunder Bay. Just as we were pulling out, Susan jumped into the front seat of the truck beside me. We sat side by side in painful silence.

At the airport in Toronto, I hopped out of the truck, thanked her father for the lift, and lined up at security. A few minutes later, Susan was beside me. "If this relationship means anything to you, you'll talk about this with me," she said.

"It's over," I replied, looking straight ahead. Susan left.

When I got home, I told my parents about the breakup. Susan called and talked me into coming down the next weekend to hash it out. My dad looked at me and said, "What are you going to do?"

I said, "I owe it to her to talk."

Dad said, "Seems to me you've already talked a lot. What are you going to do?"

Dad rarely gave me advice. When he did, it landed. His words led me to an unfortunate realization. Love isn't enough to make a relationship work. It seemed crazy to me. Terrifying, too, but it was true. It would be tough to cut the connection to my first true love, but I knew that Susan and I were through.

I agreed to fly down the next weekend, on standby, where I planned to tell her we would not be getting back together in person. On Friday, I arrived at the airport before 6 a.m. to get on the standby list for the last flight to Toronto in the evening. That night, there wasn't a seat available.

I called Susan to tell her, and we had a two-sentence argument followed by me hanging up, followed by me getting drunk with my friends, followed by me getting together with a beautiful artist I knew from high school, Missy. She and I started dating immediately.

I'd see Susan again. The University of Windsor offered a two-year business degree if you had an undergraduate degree. I had already signed up for it. Susan was coming back for her final year. I arrived at school in the fall, and Missy visited me a few weeks later. The next day, Susan's new boyfriend, Anthony, showed up. Susan and I lived in the same campus apartment building. Being faced with your ex everyday wasn't easy for either of us. We were cordial but kept our distance.

Nice hat, though. This isn't the road cap I wore to the Jays/Tigers breakup game in June 1986. That's long gone, too. However, I always make sure I have a nice Tigers New Era 5950 road cap. It's perfect, identical to the home cap other than the orange D and orange button.

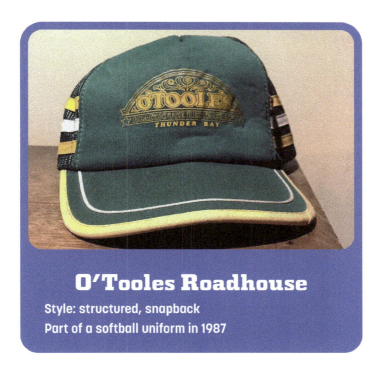

O'Tooles Roadhouse
Style: structured, snapback
Part of a softball uniform in 1987

I returned home to Thunder Bay every summer during my university years. Every Sunday morning, I'd get together with my high school friends to play baseball. About twenty of us played on a modest diamond behind a hockey arena, a short walk from my house. Foul balls would drop into the forest behind third base, often lost forever. Someone spray-painted the slogan "No Nukes" on the outfield boards, so we called it "No Nuke Park." We'd play pickup ball and talk about our Friday and Saturday night adventures.

By 1986, we were anxious to play as a real team in a real league. When I came home for Christmas, Dave and I went to different businesses looking for a sponsor. O'Tooles, a chain of roadhouse-style restaurant and bars, had just opened, and agreed to provide us with uniforms. Dave and I were selective about the roster. A fun attitude carried more weight than superior skills.

Of course, Missy was on the team. Her casual air and easy laugh led to a calm, warm relationship between us. I fell for her hard and fast. Throughout the school year, we'd written weekly and talked every Sunday morning, back when a long-distance phone bill was a serious expense to a student. Our reunions at Christmas and March Break were the highlights of the year for me. I was truly happy with Missy and thought we had a future. Unfortunately, the time apart took a toll. Our relationship collapsed under the strain of the distance. We broke up a month before I came home.

Maybe I could have mended the breach if I hadn't been so proud. I certainly had opportunities because there was no way Missy would be left off the team. She was easygoing and an incredible athlete. In high school, Missy was one of the best basketball players in the city. My friends wanted to have a good time, but they wanted to be competitive, too. I'd have to suck up my heartbreak for the summer, which I did by being emotionally distant and pretending I was fine. I wasn't. Being so near to her physically and so far away emotionally was wrenching. Still, I did my best to enjoy the team.

I'll never forget driving up to our first game, in May 1987. Our teammates were decked out in white jerseys with green lettering, green pants with gold and white piping, green stirrups, and these hats. Dave and I were giddy. We were finally a real team. We even won our first game. The summer was spent playing games in the evening, then socializing at O'Tooles. Playing softball with my friends and wearing our high school colors was a special sendoff from the place I grew up and the people I grew up with.

It was my last summer in Thunder Bay. I had one more year of university, then I would start my career. On the cusp of leaving for good, I realized that the rugged isolation of this city on the north shore of Lake Superior had become part of me. I put myself through school by working at Canada Malting, a malthouse and grain elevator on the harbor. On the way to work, I rode my bike past Hillcrest Park, with its stunning view of the Sleeping Giant, a peninsula that looks like a man lying in repose. On weekends, I'd go to the Hoito restaurant for Finnish pancakes (Thunder Bay has a large population of Finns), or eat a Persian, a pink frosted cinnamon bun unique to the Lakehead. It took a while to get there, but I had grown to love Thunder Bay.

This O'Tooles hat brings me back to that bittersweet summer. The front of our hat is foam, with a silk-screened logo. The back is plastic mesh. The cap never holds its shape. Objectively, it's terrible. Subjectively, it's beautiful.

Detroit Tigers - Home
Style: unstructured, fullback, size L
Made by Twins Enterprises, which later became '47 brand.
I have no idea when I bought it.

I was at Tiger Stadium on the last day of the 1987 regular season, when the Tigers played the Toronto Blue Jays. With a win, the Tigers would clinch the division. The weekend before, the Tigers lost three of four games in Toronto, putting Detroit three and a half games behind the Jays for first place.

With just seven games left, it looked hopeless. I was distraught. My Blue Jays fan friends were mercilessly in my face.

When they started play in 1977, the Jays were a new team in a relatively young country, their iconic split numbers were born of '70s fashion. The Blue Jays succeeded quickly, winning their division in 1985. Like Canadians, the team was always diverse and a little edgy. Anyone who thinks Canada is a country of "nice" people hasn't spent many Saturdays in a hockey arena.

The Tigers had gained some ground during the week and had a shot at winning the division in the final three game series against the dreaded Blue Jays. On Friday night, I sat in the lower deck near first base. The Tigers won 4-3. On Saturday, some university friends joined me in the bleachers to watch the Tigers beat the Jays 3-2 in the twelfth inning. This time, my classmates left depressed.

For the final showdown on Sunday, with the Tigers up by a game and a chance to win the American League East, no one would join me. So, I geared up, and lined up alone for another bleacher seat, which were sold the day of the game.

I settled into the lower deck with my scorecard. A guy from Jackson, Michigan, sat down next to me. He worked in a convenience store. None of his friends would come with him, either. If not for this game we never would have met, but for one afternoon we were best buds, high-fiving and hugging on every Tigers play.

The Tigers won 1-0 on a complete game by Tigers pitcher Frank Tanana and a solo home run by Larry Herndon, clinching the division and the best record in baseball.

When Tanana fielded a weak grounder and flipped the ball to first baseman Darrell Evans for the final out, my Jackson pal and I hugged, jumped up and down, then never saw each other again.

When I got back to my residence in Windsor, I walked down the hall singing "Take Me Out to the Ballgame." Blue Jays fans shut their doors as I walked by. Perfection.

The old-timey look of this hat reminds me of being at Tiger Stadium, my favorite place on Earth.

Montreal Expos

Style: structured, fitted
Made by New Era, 5950
Bought in 1987 at Sportsland USA, outside Tiger Stadium

The first time I wore this, I felt like I'd been traded. Not only was I wearing another team's hat, but the Expos' hat and team were the opposites of the Tigers'.

Detroit was one of the original entries to the American League in 1901. The team spanned the twentieth century, infused with baseball tradition. Their stadium predated World War I. The Tigers had worn the same home uniforms since my grandparents were young: white with a midnight olde English D and a midnight blue hat with a slightly different white olde English D. Classic. Even the name, Tigers, is iconic.

In contrast, the Expos were named after Expo 67, the International and Universal Exposition held in Montreal the year before the team was established. Their road uniforms were bright blue, white, and red, with a logo that takes a while to figure out. It's an M made from a small red "e" for Expos and a blue "b" for baseball. I swear I heard that the white part is an "l" for "les Expos Baseball" but I've never been able to confirm it. Let's just pretend it's true so that all three sections of the logo have a purpose. The hats would not look out of place on a guy in face paint making balloon animals at a kid's birthday party. But I love these hats.

I love the Expos.

When I started watching sports with my friends in high school, we watched the Expos on CBC television every Saturday night. Montreal was a great team in the 1980s. It was easy to get invested in the Kid, the Hawk, and speedy Tim Raines. We were glued to the games when they made the playoffs in 1981. The end of the final game of their series with the Dodgers ran into our senior football practice. We had to leave—not easy to do while the score was tied.

While we were tackling each other in the cold mud, Tim Cattani, my brother Scott's teammate on the junior football team, came running out of the school and onto the field, hands stretched in the air, cheering his lungs out. Everyone knew what that meant. Tim was the lone Dodgers fan at the school. He may have given us the details of Rick Monday's dramatic home run as we dragged him face first around the field. I can't quite remember. Tim was cool with it, though. His team won.

When we got older, my friends and I would go out to watch the Expos play. One local watering hole had a TV above the bar on the first floor. When the bartender saw us walking downstairs, he'd pull out our favorite beers and have them open by the time we reached the rail. My friend JohnO, a tall, fiercely opinionated ginger, hated that. He had only himself to blame for being so predictable.

The Tigers connected me to my family in Michigan, but the Expos tied me to my friends in Thunder Bay.

TSN, The Sports Network
Style: unstructured, strapback
Bought in the 1990s when I worked at TSN

After I graduated, I spent the summer contacting every television and radio station in Canada looking for a job.

In August 1988, I was hired as a reporter by CHOW, a country-and-western radio station in Welland, Ontario, a tiny town near Niagara Falls known for the system of locks that ships use to go from Lake Erie to Lake Ontario.

The job didn't go well. My reporting was good, but my on-air work was not. I was improving, but my professional development was playing chicken with my employer's patience. I was in a precarious position. The pay was just barely enough to live on. If I lost this job, I'd have to go back to Thunder Bay. While I scuffled at the radio station, I was talking to TSN, The Sports Network—a twenty-four-hour cable sports channel that went on air in 1984. I was also interviewing with New York Life to become an insurance agent.

The courtships couldn't have been more different. New York Life recruited me hard. Agents were showing me their bloated bank books and pictures of their boats. TSN just answered my calls.

In December, after four months at CHOW, two incidents changed my fate. First, I was pulled off the air as a weekend news anchor and limited to reporting, meaning my meager pay was cut further.

Then one morning I woke up to the sound of people yelling. My apartment was filled with smoke. I threw on my jacket and ran outside while the fire department entered the basement with their hose. The basement tenant sat on the stairs in her housecoat, smoking and croaking at the firefighters, "You're spraying me!"

The night before, she had pitched a still-burning cigarette butt into a pile of towels in the laundry-room sink. They were burning near a wooden wall below my bedroom. Not only was I barely making a living, but I'd had a near-death experience. I took the hint the universe was giving me. It was time to get out of that radio job.

I called both New York Life and TSN to tell them I was going to Thunder Bay for Christmas. My New York Life contact was sympathetic. My TSN contact said, "We were about to call you to tell you we'd like to put you on the schedule." That was their way of saying, "You're hired."

On January 4, 1989, I showed up for my first shift in television. Like at my Welland radio gig, the pay wasn't enough to survive on, but it was a dream job. Every night I watched sports and wrote highlight packs. No wonder they barely paid us. After a few weeks, I took a side gig at a telemarketing company during the day so I could cover my bills. I was prepared to do whatever it took to make it at TSN.

The newsroom was not a friendly place until you proved yourself, and even then, it was still a tough room. But I got my first permanent nickname, Swiss (a cheese, like my last name, Colby), and my career in television was underway.

Working in sports had benefits beyond watching games. Occasionally, we would go down to the stadium to interview players.

I carried an Al Kaline baseball card in my wallet just in case I ever had a chance to meet him. That chance came in 1992. The Tigers were in town, so I pitched a story on baseball players who had skipped the minors.

John Olerud of the Blue Jays went straight from college baseball to Major League Baseball, giving the story a local hook. Another player with this unique distinction was Al Kaline. Mr. Tiger himself. Kaline was a bonus baby in the 1950s. Because the Tigers had signed Kaline to such a large contract, he was required to start his career in the major leagues. The story was approved, so I called the SkyDome hotel. The front desk put me through to Kaline's room. I thought, *It shouldn't be this easy.* After a few rings, I heard, "Hello, this is Al Kaline." I introduced myself and told him about my story. Then I asked if he had time to talk to me today. Kaline paused, then said, sure. "Meet me by the batting cage at six o'clock."

I couldn't believe it. I was going to meet a living legend.

I immediately put on a shirt and tie and went down to SkyDome to pick up my press pass. I asked that it be available immediately. Around 1 p.m., I was on the field, waiting. There were no other members of the media present—just me, hours early, in my shirt and tie. Tigers' superstar Jack Morris practiced on the mound and looked over at me as if to say, "What the hell are you doing here?"

As the hours went by, the stadium filled, first with grounds crew, then players, then media, then fans. A colleague from TSN asked why I was there that day. I told him I was going to interview Al Kaline. He was excited for me.

I kept my eyes on the Tigers dugout. When Kaline emerged, I was going to be ready. Six o'clock came and went. My colleague said, "Maybe you should go look for him."

"No. He said he'd be here, so he will."

At 6:15, Al Kaline emerged from the Tigers dugout sporting silver hair, a sharp gray jacket, and black slacks. My heart raced a little. Then he looked around.

I thought, *Right now, Al Kaline is looking for me. He's thinking, I wonder where Craig Colby is.*

I let that sink in for a moment. Then I walked over, stuck out my hand, and said, "Hello, Mr. Kaline, I'm Craig Colby."

Kaline shook my hand and said, "Hi. I was just looking for you."

As we walked over to the cameraman, I asked Kaline about his stay in Baltimore, the Tigers stop before Toronto.

"It was great. I got to spend time with my folks." Yes, I knew he was from Baltimore.

Once Kaline was mic'ed up, we started the interview. He was taller than me, so he looked at me when I asked a question, but when he answered, he looked up and just off camera, giving me a good eyeline for my shot. Total pro.

We finished the interview, which was fantastic, then the cameraman took off the microphone. I looked Mr. Tiger in the eye, shook his hand once more, and thanked him for his time. I didn't take out the baseball card, still in my wallet. I didn't tell him I was a big fan. Either would have ruined the moment. I had something much better than ink on paper. I had a high-quality, professional exchange with one of my boyhood idols. The TSN gig was paying off.

I was so enamored with my job, I bought as much TSN gear as I could. This hat has an autumnal feel, with a thick crown and brim that look like suede. I love this logo. I'm not sure if TSN is spelled out in lights or tennis balls, but seeing this vintage branding brings me right back to the rush I felt during my salad days in television. I felt like I belonged in that room of crazed sports fans.

Chicago Cubs
Style: structure, fitted
Made by New Era, 5950
Bought at Wrigley Field in 1999

In 1990, I was promoted from editorial assistant to story editor at TSN. This meant two things. First, I could afford to live on my salary. I dropped the second job, which was taking an emotional and physical toll. I was both tired and heavy. Second, I could take a vacation.

I planned a trip to Chicago with Dave Hagberg, and some TSN friends—slim and serious show producer Mark Milliere, bearded and gregarious radio producer Rod Nystrom, and athletic and chatty Paul Jones, a high school vice-principal who worked on the Blue Jays shows in the summer. In a sign of what the media was like at the time, Paul was one of only two Black people in the newsroom. The other was his brother Mark, an on-air personality.

As hard-core baseball fans, we needed to see Comiskey Park. It was the last season for the oldest stadium in baseball at the time. We also needed to see Wrigley Field, another stadium built before World War II.

We rented a van and left Toronto in the early evening after Paul finished work. We drove through the night, listening to WFAN—New York City's all-sports radio station—on the way. A man with a heavy New York accent read baseball scores as we zipped across Michigan toward Chicago. Light was breaking as we arrived. Skyscrapers filled the clear morning sky. For us, Chicago was Sports Oz, filled with places of legend. We couldn't wait to take it all in.

After a quick nap, we pulled out a huge TSN sign about half our height—the kind used at stadiums—then created an "On Vacation" banner to attach below it. The Blue Jays were playing the White Sox and TSN was covering the game. Our friend Doug "Shakey" Walton was the Jays statistician. We told him where we were sitting so they could get a shot of us late in the game. We ate some Chicago deep-dish pizza, then set out for old Comiskey Park. We arrived early to take it all in.

The White Sox play on the south side of town, known for its tough, blue-collar neighborhoods. Migrants from the Deep South and Europe had settled here, lured by jobs at steel mills, factories, and meat-packing plants. We drove past spartan houses where kids held signs that said, "Parking $5." Paul drove past them and said, "Nice try. I'm not getting our van jacked." He had a point. The parking spots were cheap, far from the stadium, and completely unsupervised.

We parked in a big lot across from Comiskey's gleaming white façade and approached the hallowed ground. This was the first stadium built for baseball. Inside, souvenir stands were tucked within white-painted concrete caves. When we walked out to the field, behind home plate, we were transported to baseball paradise. The field was beveled at the corners and the 1950s scoreboard was straight ahead. Pillars in the lower deck put the upper deck on top of the field, making the space feel cozy. Arches were cut into the brick on the back wall of the stadium, revealing the trees outside. It was like being at a game and in a glade at the same time. I gasped. It was gorgeous.

We walked around the stadium, then found our seats down the leftfield line. The White Sox were wearing crisp white uniforms with White Sox written in navy blue script trimmed in red across the chest. Their hats were navy with a red brim and a lower-case cursive C in white with red trim. The look fit with the old stadium, but the White Sox always seemed to have an unusual relationship with their history.

They were charter members of the American League, which formed in 1901, but they'd only won two World Championships: in 1906 and 1917. The south siders' biggest claim to fame was suspending eight players, including Shoeless Joe Jackson, for throwing the 1919 World Series to the Reds. It seemed like shame had made them twitchy.

Over the years, they wore some of the ugliest uniforms in the game's history, including, very briefly, Bermuda shorts, and polyester pajama pullovers popular in the 1970s, with SOX written on a big blue bar between two small red bars.

No team loved gimmicks more. In 1979, the White Sox forfeited the second game of a doubleheader to the Tigers because the field had been damaged when boxes of disco records were blown up after the first game on Disco Demolition night.

As a franchise, the White Sox seemed uncomfortable, insecure. Fortunately, some of their luster had returned thanks to the movie *Field of Dreams*, released in 1989, which romanticized Shoeless Joe Jackson.

We saw a good game, with the Jays winning 4-3 and the TSN broadcast showed us with our big sign. The experience was epic, and the trip was just getting started.

After the game, we went to pick up Shakey. He and the rest of the TSN production team were staying at the same hotel as the Blue Jays. As we waited for Shakey, their star leftfielder George Bell walked into the lobby. During the game, he had chewed out a ball girl stationed down the leftfield line. I yelled out, "Hey, George, what did you say to the ball girl?" He told us that the ball girl didn't move her metal stool out of the way when he was chasing a fly ball toward the stands. He could have been injured. Bell's retelling of the encounter was filled with a colorful descriptor.

That night we went to the Baha Beach Club, which was surprisingly busy on a Monday night. At one point in the evening, all the waitresses stopped what they were doing and danced in unison on the tables. While we were talking, a large hand appeared around Paul Jones's neck. The hand was attached to Blue Jays pitcher David Wells.

Wells recognized Paul from his work on the Blue Jays weekly show. He hung around with us for about fifteen minutes. This capper to the evening was beyond our expectations. We knew we'd see games in classic stadiums. Mixing with athletes and a floor show that tapped into our late twenties' testosterone energized us. We should have been exhausted after driving all night from Toronto. Nope. We went to bed at 4 a.m.

We got up just four hours later to have breakfast then head to our next destination on the north side of Chicago, Wrigley Field. Unlike Comiskey Park's gritty south-side setting, Wrigley had a party-like atmosphere. Charming little bars lined the streets around the stadium. Tables selling souvenirs were everywhere.

Inside this friendly neighborhood stadium was a pastoral paradise. The pristine green grass of the outfield flowed into ivy-covered walls. The park felt both warm and important. Despite decades of poor play by the Cubs, their stadium was still a prime destination. Unlike the White Sox, the Cubs knew exactly who they were—lovable losers.

In the forty-five seasons between their last World Series appearance—a loss to my Tigers in 1945—they posted a losing record thirty-three times. They'd have a losing record this year, too. Yet, somehow, they'd made poor play part of their charm. You weren't going to the game to see them win. You were going to have a great time. I'm sure Cubs fans were frustrated, but they still showed up. The Cubs took the field in white uniforms with royal blue pinstripes and the classic blue hat with the friendly red C surrounded by a white trim.

Our seats were in the bleachers. I often score the game but keeping score in the Wrigley Field bleachers was like trying to do homework at a toga party. By the middle of the game, we were talking about Canadian bands with some new best friends, a group of guys about our age who skipped out of work. A few minutes later, we were singing "These Eyes" by the Guess Who at the top of our lungs. By the late innings, I was vaguely aware a game was being played out there somewhere. After the game, we went to Cubby Bears, a bar across the street from the stadium, where one of our new friends ran into his boss. We didn't see them again.

Fortunately, before the disappearance, our new best friends told us we needed to go to Kingston Mines that night, a north-side blues club. Rod, Dave, and I did, while Paul and Mark opted for the clubs downtown. We took our seats at old wooden chairs in front of a modest stage. A young man in a blue T-shirt and jeans started playing guitar and singing "My Babe," Little Walter's blues classic. He was fantastic.

Then a man in his fifties, in grey dress pants and a silky shirt, stepped up and belted out "Knock on Wood" in front of a full band and blew the roof off the place. Once he was finished, a band came onto a stage on the other side of the bar. We heard stellar blues performances all night long. The bar was open until 4 a.m., but we only made it to three in the morning. Our heads were spinning. We were surfing on waves of A+ experiences.

At 8 a.m., we were up for breakfast, reading each other headlines from "The National," a new sports daily paper. Then it was time for a Chicago baseball doubleheader.

Our first stop was Wrigley Field for an afternoon game. From the upper deck on the first base side, we could see parties on rooftops across the street. Young people were watching the game, grilling burgers, and drinking beer. The binoculars I brought were repurposed between innings to watch the pretty women in their neon tops. Whoever was manning the field lenses would give us an update

At one point, Paul Jones said, "The blonde woman in the pink top is pouring a beer and giving it to Dave Stiff." We looked at Paul in disbelief. Dave Stiff was the TSN social butterfly. We had no idea he was in town, let alone at a Cubs rooftop party. After the game, we went to the building and called up to Dave. He waved, then came down.

Dave had been served more than one beer. He was in town for a fraternity convention. As a connoisseur of festive gatherings, Dave had done a feature on the rooftop parties surrounding the Cubs games earlier in the year. As a party opportunist, he just happened to drop off a VHS copy of the story right before game time. Of course, he was invited up. I had to admire his chutzpah.

That night, we saw the White Sox play the Jays again at Comiskey, sitting on the first-base side in the lower deck, talking to a woman who had dated one of the Chicago Blackhawks. She was surprised that we knew so much about him. No big deal. We were paid to know those things. After the game, we waited for

Shakey outside the production truck. He had a present for us: a cup of Comiskey Park dirt he'd scooped out of the infield. Back at the hotel, we carefully divided the treasure. And, yes, I still have my share.

That night we went to Excalibur, a downtown dance club. Some of the White Sox were on the dance floor. There were more beautiful women in that place than anywhere I had ever been in my twenty-eight years. On top of that, the club was hosting the finals of the bikini contest. Dave and I just looked at each other. He said, "We can never tell anyone about this. They won't believe us." From then on, we called Excalibur "the Unspeakable Place." Before the night was over, some students from North Carolina taught us an unofficial version of the school fight song that ended with "Go to hell, State!" and I kissed a Chicago girl.

The next day we went up the Sears Tower then drove to Chicago Stadium, home of Michael Jordan and the Chicago Bulls. We talked some security guards into letting us on the floor. The basketball court was set up. For hard-core sports fans, it was like being in an empty cathedral. My imagination filled in Michael Jordan soaring to the hoop for a thunderous jam, the crowd rising to its feet in response. That energy was still in the building, hanging in the air like a ghost.

On the way back to Toronto, we stopped in Detroit to see the Brewers play the Tigers. I bribed an usher to put us three rows behind home plate. The Tigers were losing late in the game when some of our neighbors started to leave. Tigers' catcher Mike Heath turned around and yelled, "Where are you going? The game's not over yet!" The five of us were in no hurry to leave this sports-fan heaven. Sadly, the Tigers lost.

For me, at least, this was more than a vacation. It was a journey to different cultures, exploring the habitats of other sports fans. Their everyday atmosphere was fresh air to me. I'd go on sports trips again, but it would never be like this. Other than Rod—who was married, with a wife expecting their first child—we were all single. Sports were everything to us. This was a young man's adventure, the kind I could never have when life's true priorities claimed me.

I bought a Cubs hat on this trip and wore it until it lost its shape. I picked up the hat in this picture on a subsequent trip because I love the Cubs cap. The bright palette and simple design reflect the joyous experience of an afternoon at Wrigley Field. The colors are red, white, and blue, but my hat also has the golden tinge of youth.

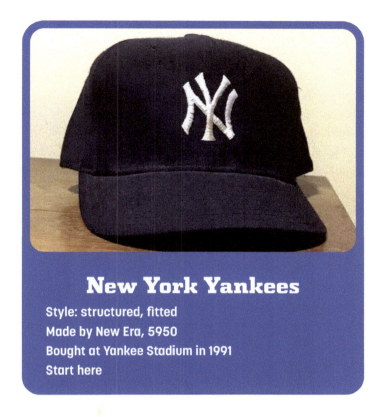

New York Yankees

Style: structured, fitted
Made by New Era, 5950
Bought at Yankee Stadium in 1991
Start here

When my brother Jim got a job in the Big Apple and moved to Connecticut, my parents and I drove to New York City.

Mom, Dad, and I spent a day walking around Manhattan, a huge thrill. New York was exactly like I'd imagined: huge buildings, rushing people, honking cabs. The Yankees were at home, so I asked my parents if they wanted to go to the game. The answer was a qualified "yes."

Mom asked, "How will we get there?"

I asked the woman at the information booth at Grand Central Station. She said, "No problem, the No. 4 subway stops right at the stadium."

I relayed this to my parents. "Getting there is easy," And I shared the details.

"I don't know. It could be dangerous," Mom replied. "Ask the lady if it's dangerous."

To reassure Mom, I went back to the woman at the information booth. "Is the No. 4 line safe? I'm with my parents."

She said, "Millions of people ride the subway every day. You'll be fine."

I walked back to Mom and told her, "She says millions of people ride the subway every day. We'll be fine. Let's go. It's no big deal."

Mom was unconvinced. "Maybe we should take a cab. Pete, what do you think? Should we take a cab?"

I said, "Mom, the subway will be fine."

Mom said, "Go ask the lady at information if we'd be better off taking a cab."

"Mom, she already said it was safe!"

"Just ask her."

I slunk back to the information desk. "My mother wants to know if we'd be safer taking a cab than the subway."

The information desk lady looked at me blankly for a second. Then she said, "You're a man. Be a man."

I stomped back to Mom and declared, "We're taking the subway!"

Five minutes later, we were in a cab.

Yankee Stadium was magical. It oozed history. The Yankees are more than a baseball team. They're icons of American achievement. The Yankees are corporate and cocky; winning is expected. Their bar starts with excellence. I admire that.

Their logo is the picture of symmetry. The white on dark blue is classy and confident. The home whites with pinstripes are impeccable and the road jerseys—gray with block New York in blue surrounded by white—are subtle and efficient. The Yankees get a tip of their classic hat for not putting names on the back of their jerseys. It's not about the individual in the Bronx, it's about the team.

The stadium itself felt like an idealized version of America. The upper deck facing was a classic arched, white-picket fence. The grass glowed under the stadium lights. It was impossible not to imagine Babe Ruth, Lou Gehrig, and Reggie Jackson in the batter's box.

Proposals posted on the scoreboard between innings were written casually, "Yo, Maria, marry me already! Love, Tony." The announcer's reading of them, however, was formal. "Tony asks Maria if she would like to marry him." The Yankee Stadium experience was a mix of uptown and downtown. In the bathrooms, the urinals were huge troughs. Honestly, some of the New Yorkers could have used coaching on minimizing splashback. Otherwise, the Yankee Stadium experience was perfect.

We sat in the 200 level between home and first. The Yankees beat the Angels 7-1. Former Tigers caught for both teams. Lance Parrish on the Angels and Matt Nokes was on the Yankees. Nokes homered. I managed to talk my parents into taking the subway back from the game, but only after Mom forced me to ask a cop if we'd be OK. "Stand next to the conductor," he told us. To placate Mom, we did.

I bought this cap at the stadium. You can tell it's old because the lettering isn't raised. It's also been worn so much that the logo is a little sweat stained.

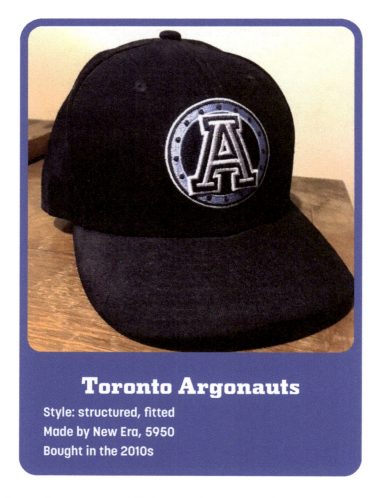

Toronto Argonauts
Style: structured, fitted
Made by New Era, 5950
Bought in the 2010s

The Argos became my CFL team when I moved to Toronto. The timing was perfect. In 1991, John Candy, Wayne Gretzky, and Bruce McNall bought the team. They immediately signed Heisman Trophy-winning receiver Raghib "Rocket" Ismail out of Notre Dame to a four-year, $18.2-million contract. The Argos became a sensation. I worked at the games occasionally, and once ran into John Candy.

The Argos players created a regular half-time skit, which they'd shoot at the TSN studio. I saw Rocket sitting in the hallway writing a script while we were getting ready to record *Sportsdesk*. By far my favorite Argonaut, and probably my favorite Toronto athlete, was Michael "Pinball" Clemons, a multipurpose back who caught passes and returned kicks. Pinball set the single-season CFL record for all-purpose yards in 1990.

One day when we were getting ready for the morning meeting, I was sitting with my friend Geoff Macht, a fellow story editor, and my boss Mike Day, planning the show. I saw Pinball in the newsroom, so I said to the group, "See Pinball Clemons out there? Give him a football five yards away and I'll tackle him every time."

My boss said, "Really?"

I replied, "Oh yeah! I was the captain of my high school football team." I thought everyone would know I was joking. There was no way I could even get a hand on Clemons.

Mike launched out of his chair. "I'm setting it up!" Before I could make a sound, Mike was in the newsroom, shaking Pinball's hand. I could see them talking. Mike waved me into the conversation.

"Pinball, this is Swiss. He said that if you had a football five yards away from him, he could tackle you every time."

Pinball looked up at me (he's about five feet six inches). I knew that this would end with grass stains on my good clothes and a story that would haunt me forever. Pinball was silent for a moment. I was resigned to imminent humiliation.

Then Pinball said, "He probably could."

That was one of the classiest and smartest moves I'd ever seen. In three words, he let me off the hook. He also dodged the possibility of being injured if the dufus in front of him got lucky.

After that, Pinball would say hi to me whenever he saw me in the office. Once he complimented my football tie. I still regret not giving it to him on the spot.

Go Argos!

I think of Pinball every time I put on this excellent Argos New Era 5950. The team has had a variety of cool logos—a strong-armed warrior with a shield, a boat shaped like a football, with oars poking out of the side—but this strong-looking A mounted in a circle suggestive of a battle shield is my favorite. It has a little majesty. The iconic double-blue color scheme is nice, too.

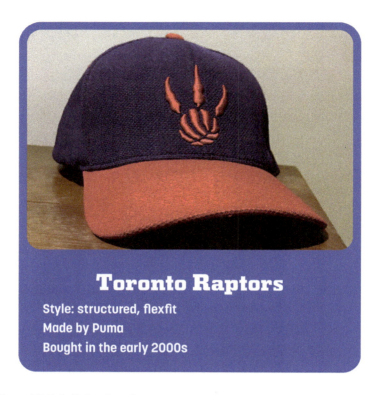

Toronto Raptors

Style: structured, flexfit
Made by Puma
Bought in the early 2000s

In May 1994, I had a decision to make. Toronto was going to get an NBA team. They announced the name: the Raptors. They'd start playing the following year. The decision was—should I become a Raptors fan?

I already had a favorite basketball team, the Detroit Pistons. The Bad Boy Pistons won back-to-back championships three years earlier by playing tough defense and being selfless. I adored those teams. Giving up that fealty was almost impossible to imagine. Cutting ties with Detroit had other implications. Like all immigrants, I held onto certain things that tied me to my former home. For me, those ties were the Detroit sports teams. Giving up one meant discarding part of my identity.

Becoming a Raptors fan meant acknowledging that I was now part of Toronto. As an immigrant, it can take a long time to feel like you belong, if you ever do. However, I'd been in the city five years and had no plans to leave. This team was starting a life in Toronto, just like me. That was enough to tip the scales. I decided to belong in Toronto. I went with the Purple Dinosaurs.

I bought a shirt with the dino logo as soon as it went on sale. In the Raptors' first season, 1995-1996, I attended my first game with my best friend, Dave.

It took me a few years to buy a hat though. I like this one because of the purple-and-red color scheme (I loved it when purple was the Raptors dominant color) and this is my favorite Raptors logo. Why do so many NBA logos have a basketball in them? Yeah, you're a basketball team. We get it already.

Thunder Bay Whiskey Jacks - Home
Style: structured, snapback
Bought in 1993, the first year of the team's existence.

In 1993, the citizens of Thunder Bay got a new team, too: a professional minor league baseball team named the Whiskey Jacks. People were thrilled. At the first game, demand for tickets was great but owner Ricky May didn't turn anyone away. Overflow fans stood on the warning track at Port Arthur Stadium, a nondescript field used for football and baseball. The rest sat in a modest concrete grandstand.

The Jacks played in the Northern League, which wasn't affiliated with Major League Baseball, but was still plenty exciting. Former Major Leaguers signed on to teams in the league—notably the Saints from St. Paul, Minnesota. Stars like Pedro Guerrero, Darryl Strawberry and Jack Morris were competing on the same field where I played high school football. My best friend Dave told me about Darryl Strawberry's first at-bat at Port Arthur Stadium. The first pitch was ball one. The second pitch was the longest home run he'd ever seen. It left Port Arthur Stadium and cleared another baseball diamond beyond rightfield, too.

I saw the Jacks when I came home on vacation later in the summer. TSN sent my good friend Lisa Bowes, their Winnipeg reporter, to do a story on the team. That's how buzzworthy the Jacks were. While Lisa was in town, I hung around with her crew while she did the story. It was fun to meet the owner and players. Mostly, it was a thrill to go home and see good baseball.

The Whiskey Jacks also had a cool name and fantastic colors. Teal and purple felt very hip for industrial Thunder Bay. The gray bird perched on a bat in front of the arched TB was a classic baseball look. The combination was irresistible. The hats were a huge hit in Thunder Bay. It seemed like everybody in town had one. This hat is misshapen because I wore it so often.

Baltimore Orioles

Style: Structured, fitted
Made by New Era, 5950
Bought at Camden Yards in 1994.

My best friend Dave had a new girlfriend, Relita Misa, whom he met at work. Dave was the executive director of the Kairos Community Resource Centre, an open custody facility for youths in the criminal justice system. He helped troubled kids try to get back into society. Relita worked there, too. Of course, I was anxious to meet her, so Scott and I scheduled drinks with Relita and Dave when we were back in Thunder Bay.

Dave told Relita to be prepared to be interviewed. Dave was right. Scott and I asked a lot of questions.

"Where did you meet?"

"What do you do at Kairos?"

"What's your favorite movie?"

Being Dave's girlfriend was a big deal. We wanted to get to know Relita.

She not only survived the inquisition, but she impressed both of us. Dave was always popular with women. He had his choice, and he could not have chosen better than this vivacious, pretty, smart, funny brunette. Relita was kind and wonderful in every way there is to be. She could also needle with the best of them.

At their wedding in the fall of 1992, Scott was the emcee and I was the best man. It was one of the best weekends of my life.

In 1994, Dave, Relita, and I planned a baseball trip that was to include my girlfriend Wendy, a petite, cute elementary school teacher with a light brown bob cut. A few weeks before we left, she bailed on the trip. She may not have been thrilled about the idea of spending a week driving on highways and sitting in baseball parks. More likely, she could see our relationship coming to an end.

We'd been dating for a year. For her birthday a few months earlier, I'd given her a gold chain. My birthday would happen on the trip. Before we left, she gave me my present—a cassette-tape soundtrack to the movie "The Coneheads." It was a frivolous gift, reflective of where she saw our relationship. She wasn't wrong. I liked Wendy a lot, but we vibrated at different frequencies. She was too nervous for me, and I was too intense for her.

The truth was that, despite dating some impressive women, I hadn't been truly happy in a relationship since I was with Missy seven years earlier. I knew the breakup was coming when I got back to Toronto. However, we still listened to the soundtrack on the trip. It was pretty good.

The first stop was New York City, where we saw the Yankees play the Red Sox. There was a rain delay that soaked the stadium. After the rain passed, we returned to our seats, smack dab in the middle of a group of drunk Long Island cops. The most obnoxious guy passed out late in the game, so his friends made him a hat from waterlogged cup holders and huge beer cups. We waved to the centerfield cameraman, who whipped his camera around to share an image of the cop's cup cap with the 30,000 other fans in attendance. His friends howled with laughter. The shot was on CNN that night, too.

Then we were off to Baltimore, home of Dave's favorite team, the Orioles. Relita's brother Reynaldo, a travel agent, flew in from Toronto to join us on this leg of the trip. He was well suited to the job. There didn't seem to be a destination or experience that didn't intrigue Reynaldo.

Orioles Park at Camden Yards was just a few years old, but it felt like a throwback. The designers had rejected the cookie-cutter, multipurpose stadiums of the 1960s and 1970s to create an idealized place to watch this beautiful game. At the time, this unique venue was as much an attraction as the game itself.

The modern-day conveniences of wide concourses and luxury boxes mingled with old-fashioned brick and steel. The upper decks opened in centerfield to reveal Baltimore's modest skyline. Just beyond rightfield is a promenade between the seats and the classic B&O Warehouse. The stadium is just two blocks from Babe Ruth's birthplace.

The Orioles were a winning team born of losing. In 1954, the sad-sack St. Louis Browns moved to Baltimore and wisely renamed themselves, embracing a nickname Baltimore had used in the nineteenth-century. They started winning big time in the 1960s and 1970s with teams built on the Oriole Way: pitching, defense, and the three-run homer. Unfortunately, that personality has been lost.

We saw a couple of good games while we were there. Devon White of the Blue Jays made the greatest catch I've ever seen, folding himself over the centerfield wall to rob a home run. We also saw Cal Ripken's 1,999th consecutive game. Of course, the video tribute was set to Prince's *1999*.

Baltimore's orange-and-black color scheme stand out in contrast to the traditional uniforms of East Coast rivals like the Yankees and Red Sox. The Orioles' uniforms have varied from wacky—orange bottoms and pajama-pullover tops with a smirking cartoon bird logo—to classic button-up tops with black-script "Orioles" trimmed in orange topped with a black cap and an ornithologically correct bird. Somehow, the Orioles pull off both looks.

I love this Orioles hat. The lifelike bird fits well with the pastoral imagery of baseball, particularly in this classically styled stadium, and is both stately and vibrant. For some reason, this New Era 5950 fits really well.

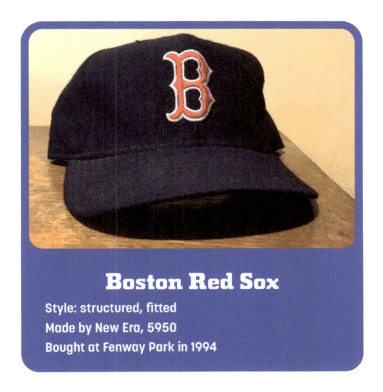

Boston Red Sox

Style: structured, fitted
Made by New Era, 5950
Bought at Fenway Park in 1994

Our last stop on the trip was Boston. Reynaldo thought about going back to Toronto. We stopped outside the airport long enough for Reynaldo to stare at his luggage, motionless, for a few minutes. Eventually, I closed the trunk and said, "Let's go." Reynaldo hopped in the car.

The defining characteristic of the Red Sox in the twentieth century was heartbreak. Like their bitter archrivals, the New York Yankees, the Red Sox had a tradition built on legendary players, winning regular seasons and a classic ballpark. Unlike the Yankees, the Red Sox legacy also included spectacular collapses that had denied them a championship since 1918, when they were led by star pitcher Babe Ruth, soon to be sold to the Yankees. They had won three World Series with the Babe, and none since he was shipped out. The Curse of the Bambino hung over the franchise. Red Sox fans had earned the chip on their shoulders.

Entering Fenway Park was like stepping inside a legend. It was the last of the pre-World War I stadiums I had yet to visit. Fenway has the most unusual quirk in the game, a big green wall in leftfield to compensate for the inability to acquire more land to build a bigger stadium. The concourses felt like the ones in Tiger Stadium and old Comiskey Park, spare and dimly lit. The decades surrounded me.

Baseball fans are supposed to love Fenway Park. I wanted to, but I didn't. Some of the fans around us were extra obnoxious, which was Dave's biggest takeaway from Fenway. Still, I'm glad I went. I'm especially glad I bought this Red Sox New Era 5950 cap. Simplicity and elegance are the keys to a classic baseball hat and the Red Sox cap epitomizes that. The stylish Red B with an understated white trim looks at home on the dark blue field. Beautiful. One of the classiest hats in the game, it looks and feels like baseball.

We had seats in the bleachers, looking right into the visiting team's bullpen, for a doubleheader against the Blue Jays. After the games, we had a beer in one of the many great pubs near the stadium. We saw a game the next day, too, from seats out in rightfield.

We drove back to Toronto, listening to "The Coneheads" soundtrack and "The Jerky Boys," a tape my brother Jim gave me for my thirty-first birthday, which we celebrated in Baltimore. The Jerky Boys were a pair of comedians who made crank calls as different characters. It was hilarious. Relita, Reynaldo, and I still call each other "tough guy"—a phrase used frequently on the tape. By far the best part of the trip was getting to know my best friend's wife and brother-in-law better. Dave was family to me and now they were, too.

When I got home, Wendy and I broke up. There was no drama. We both knew we didn't have a future together. Even worse, and far less amicable, the MLB players went on strike, wiping out the World Series for the first time in ninety years.

I was so mad I didn't go to a Major League Baseball game in 1995 when they resumed play.

The Discovery Channel
Style: unstructured, strapback
Bought in the early 1990s.

I never thought I'd leave TSN. Still, in 1994, I had to consider it. Office politics were working against me, and, just six years into my career I was teaching, not learning. The leadership at TSN had bought the Canadian rights to the Discovery Channel and were starting to staff up for a daily science news show. I applied for a job as a producer, and they hired me.

Leaving TSN was tough. It was also one of the best decisions I've ever made. The Discovery Channel office was in the same building as TSN. Our desks were on the fourth floor, while TSN was on the first. The difference involved more than just geography. The workplace was largely female, a stark contrast to the male-dominated, locker-room atmosphere at TSN.

I remember hearing two colleagues talking about wearing brown shoes with black pants. "I wasn't sure it was a good idea, but my friend told me, 'Just go ahead and do it!' and she was right! I loved it!" I hadn't heard conversations like that at work before.

Also, most of my new workmates were married, unlike the predominantly single staff at TSN. The change was good for me. I was now thirty-one. My perspectives had to broaden. I wanted a different work life, and I was getting even more than I had expected. Meeting coworkers with different life experiences was exhilarating.

The staff on "@discovery.ca" (the show was named after our e-mail address) came from diverse backgrounds. There were science journalists from CBC Radio's science show "Quirks and Quarks," a few people from CBC news, one from a CTV morning show, and the daughter of a Nobel Prize winner in physics. Everyone brought a different skill, which was essential to create a show unlike any other in the world. No one else was creating an hour of science programming every day.

I made new friends, including fellow sports fan Larry Bambrick. Larry, a senior producer on the show, sat immediately to my right. Bespectacled and slightly built with glasses, he had an affable, professorial air. It wasn't unusual for Larry to burst into song when he walked down the hall. He was also a natural athlete. We would often drive our co-worker crazy as we threw a Nerf ball around the office.

Executive producer Paul Lewis, an intelligent man with a soft-spoken wit, moved opportunities around the staff to minimize rivalries. Every morning we talked about the previous night's show, so feedback on your work was built into the routine. Every day I learned. At Discovery Channel, I grew into a full producer.

The best days on the job were the best days on any job. The best of all was in the fall of 1996, when I was sent to Cleveland with our new host, Gill Deacon. Gill was clever, with a disarming friendliness. We reported to NASA Glenn Research Center (I had no idea there was a NASA base in Cleveland) and met a flight crew, camera crew, representatives from the Canadian Space Agency (CSA), and Canadian astronaut Bjarni Tryggvason.

Bjarni had been assigned to a Space Shuttle flight the following summer. To promote that, the CSA had invited us to join him for an adventure on a version of the famous Vomit Comet, an airplane that simulates weightlessness by flying up like a roller coaster then tipping the nose down and falling. The drop lasts about twenty seconds.

While the plane, and everything in it falls, you feel weightless, relative to your surroundings. Of course, you're not actually weightless or the pilot wouldn't have to pull the nose up to prevent a fiery death. Ron Howard used the original Vomit Comet in Houston to shoot the weightless scenes of the movie "Apollo 13."

Gill and I were given some forest-green flight suits and medicine to prevent motion sickness. We were told that two out of three people will be sick, one mildly, one severely. The other lucky person isn't sick at all. Then we were shown how to properly throw up on the plane: You throw up in a paper bag, then seal it in a plastic Ziploc bag.

The plane took off and flew to the sky over Michigan where we would take our roller-coaster flight. There were some seats in the back of the plane, but most were removed to make room for science experiments. That's the real purpose of these flights. One of the reasons Bjarni was going to space was to test his Microgravity Isolation Mount, a device designed to prevent experiments from being affected by vibrations on the Space Shuttle or the soon-to-be-launched International Space Station.

We were instructed to secure any bags or jackets with a seatbelt, so they didn't float off when we're falling or fall down when the nose of the plane is pulled up.

As we approached our first nosedive, our camera crew took their positions, and Gill stood next to Bjarni so that we could capture her reaction to losing the grip of gravity. Gill had just started on the show. I'd never been on a shoot with her, so I didn't know her personally or professionally yet.

On the plane, weightlessness begins and ends with the sound of a bell. The bell rang and my feet left the floor. The sensation was like being on the back of a roller coaster as it comes out of a valley and flies over the top of a rise, where you float out of your seat for a microsecond. It's also a bit like swimming completely submerged but without the pressure of water.

I'm sure I laughed as my weight seemed to vanish, but I tried to suppress the euphoria because I was working. I turned my attention to Gill to see her reaction. Gill's eyes widened, her jaw dropped, and she started breathing quickly. It was a genuine reaction that embodied the feeling we were all experiencing. Gill perfectly showed our viewers what the sensation was like.

A NASA employee in a blue jumpsuit put his hand on my shoulder and whispered in my ear, "Don't do that." I didn't realize it, but I was kicking my feet as though I was under water. Not only was it a useless gesture, but I could hurt someone. I apologized just before the bell rang. It was time to get my feet underneath me to avoid falling on my face.

We recorded some more video of Gill enjoying the experience. A NASA crewman squeezed a plastic bottle releasing a jiggling ball of water that Gill consumed as it floated in the cabin. A photographer took a picture of Bjarni holding Gill and me up by the ankles. Then I started capturing scenes I could edit together later. Usually, I would have structured the story and mapped out everything we needed to shoot but I had no idea what to expect from the experience, so I was flying by the seat of my pants.

The cameraman's face was turning the same shade of green as his jumpsuit. Looking through a camera lens heightens the disorientation you feel while you're weightless, making it even more likely that you'll throw up. He was the one of three that was really sick.

At one point, I needed Gill for a shot, so I floated over to her and said, "Hey Gill." She smiled, held up her finger to indicate she needed a moment, then barfed into a paper bag. She popped that bag into the Ziploc baggie and sealed it like a pro. Then she asked me a question I've never been asked by a host before or since. "Did I barf off all my lipstick?" She hadn't. And she was in good spirits. Gill was the one in three that was mildly sick.

I was working a smaller second camera, but that didn't make me feel nauseous. I also looked out the window, another disorienting trigger for sickness. Nothing. I was upside down a couple of times, too, another way to bring on a good barfing. It turns out I was the one in three who was not sick at all. I was free to enjoy the ride. At least as much as I could while still trying to work.

Finally, after fifty parabolas over my home state of Michigan, the final twenty seconds of weightlessness was announced. I took in every wonderful moment. Finally, the bell rang, and gravity resumed its dominion over us. Gill yelled, "Yay! Craigy makes no vomit!" Then she said what both of us were thinking: "I can't believe we'll never be weightless again."

That was one of my best days at work. It was also a bonding experience with Gill, perhaps the most natural on-camera host I've ever worked with and a wonderful human being.

I loved working at Discovery Channel.

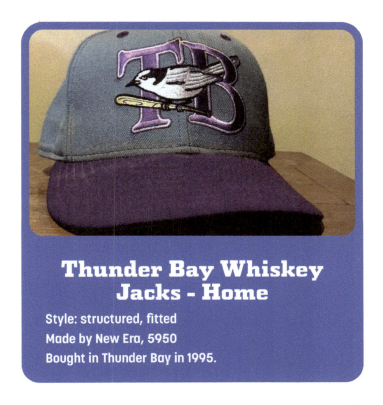

Thunder Bay Whiskey Jacks - Home

Style: structured, fitted
Made by New Era, 5950
Bought in Thunder Bay in 1995.

In May 1995, Laura Boast invited me to her thirtieth birthday party. Laura became an extended family member when she worked with Scott at *the Chronicle Journal* in Thunder Bay. She was cute and curvy with shoulder-length brown hair. Laura burst with energy, opinions, huge laughs, and big hugs. She was a Colby by nature, if not blood. This honorary family member was celebrating her milestone in her hometown, Toronto.

The party was at her mother's co-op apartment in downtown Toronto near Bay and Bloor. I walked into her mother's apartment, looked into the kitchen, and saw this slim, pretty woman with blonde hair, rushing around, focused on the preparations. My first thought was: *Wow, who's she?*

Her name was Nancy Adderley. Nancy met Laura when she worked at the Thunder Bay CBC radio station as a reporter. She was wearing a floral peasant blouse with tan slacks. Her hair fell to her shoulders, her nose was pointed and perfect, and the bottom half of her face looked like a valentine.

We chatted a bit. Nancy had left the CBC for a communications job with the Canada Mortgage and Housing Corporation. She was in town on a three-month work project. Once the party moved to the co-op's common courtyard, I worked the barbecue and Nancy joined the group at the table.

When dinner was over, it was time to turn off the grill. There were two propane tanks underneath the barbecue, and I followed the hose to see which to turn off. I reached in to turn off the gas. WHOOSH! When I touched the propane tank valve, a ball of flame engulfed the barbecue.

I yanked my hand out. Was my skin charred? Was my jacket on fire? Good on both counts. But the entire barbecue was a huge fireball. There was no way I could turn off the valve. I looked around for a fire extinguisher. Surely a shared barbecue would have one nearby. Nope. I looked for a hose. Nope. A bucket? Nope. A tarp or anything to smother the flames? Nothing. My thin windbreaker would melt if I used that.

Someone yelled, "Call the fire department!" People looked over the fence from a restaurant patio, smiling and laughing. No help there. Maybe there was a hose closer to the building. As I looked back, I saw Nancy coming out of the co-op with a fire extinguisher. I ran over to her. She asked, "Do you know how to use this?"

I did. This may seem like an odd time for a sidebar, but this one is germane to the story. When I was seven years old, my family was driving in our wood-paneled station wagon to see my grandparents. My brothers Scott, five, and Jim, ten, and I sat in the far back of the vehicle. The floor pulled open to create two facing benches. We were playing with little plastic spacemen. Jim pointed to a fire extinguisher stowed in the back and said, "I dare you to set it off."

I looked at the handle. To discharge the powder, I'd have to squeeze two prongs of metal together. If I squeezed it just a bit, only a little would come out. I wouldn't have to chicken out and Mom and Dad wouldn't notice.

I removed the fire extinguisher and pulled out the pin that blocks the handle from squeezing. My parents didn't hear the noise. So far, so good. I started to apply the smallest amount of strength I could. As soon as a tiny amount of discharge escaped, I would stop. Nothing came out so far. I squeezed a little harder. Still nothing. So, I squeezed just a bit more. WHOOSH! A huge white cloud covered the back of the station wagon.

"WHAT THE HELL IS GOING ON BACK THERE?" my dad bellowed.

He swerved the car to the side of the highway, jumped out of the driver seat, then jerked open the rear door. Dad pulled each of us out of the vehicle. A wave of excited excuses blasted out of his three sons. Dad spanked all of us, right there on the side of the highway. Scott yelled through his tears, "But I didn't do anything!" Dad barked, "Be careful who you associate with!"

Mom and Dad mopped up the white mess as cars whizzed by in the Michigan summer heat. We got back in, and the car pulled out. Scott and I were still shaken. A different cloud hung in the back of the station wagon: tension. Then Jim picked up two spacemen, one covered in white powder and one clean. He said "OK, the ones with white stuff on them are dead."

So when Nancy asked, "Do you know how to use this?" I just said yes.

I grabbed the fire extinguisher and rushed back to the ball of flame. I pulled the pin and emptied the contents onto the blaze. It took the full container to put out the fire. You could still hear the gas hissing in the night air.

The fire department showed up and waved us all back. We retreated about six feet. They said, "No, go back into the building." We did.

I waited nervously. What had I done to start the fire? I'd barely touched the tank. Finally, a fireman walked up with a piece of metal. He said it was the part at the end of the hose that was supposed to screw into the propane tank. It was so old that the threading was stripped. It couldn't be screwed in, so people had just plugged it in and hoped for the best. I cheered, "It wasn't my fault."

What they said next chilled my blood. "It turned out all right because you put out the fire, but you really shouldn't have done that. You should have left and called us to deal with it."

"What could have happened?"

"The tank could have exploded. Or the one next to it could have."

"What would have happened then?"

"You'd all be dead."

There was a moment of silence as we absorbed that thought. We had been a coin flip away from death.

Then we went upstairs for cake.

Laura opened cards that were eerily in line with the night's excitement: cakes with forests of burning candles, jokes about calling for help, things like that. Someone asked Nancy how she found the fire extinguisher. Nancy said she saw it on the way out to the courtyard and made note of where it was. Wow. Smart.

I offered to drive Nancy home. She declined. Fortunately, we had another friend in common, Lisa MacGillivray, so the three of us got together. I invited Nancy to play softball with my work team, which she did. Then her project finished, and Nancy went back to Thunder Bay. When I visited my parents in August, I saw the Whiskey Jacks four nights in a row. One night, I invited Nancy to join me. She did.

I also bought a New Era 5950 Whiskey Jacks home cap. My other cap was getting ratty, and I wanted to wear the Cadillac of hats when I cheered on my hometown team.

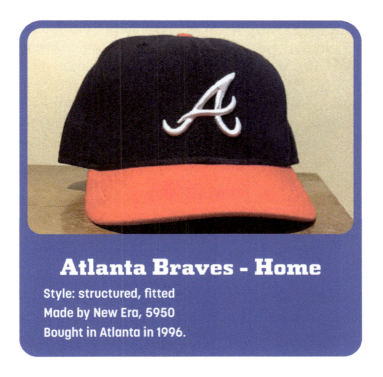

Atlanta Braves - Home
Style: structured, fitted
Made by New Era, 5950
Bought in Atlanta in 1996.

In 1996, I worked at the Atlanta Olympics as a font producer for the weightlifting events. I was responsible for all the writing on the screen—names, country of origin, and scores.

Because I was American, I could work for the host broadcaster, which provides the television feed for the world. It could not have been a sweeter gig. The contract included three weeks of rehearsals, five days of competition, a day off, and five more days of competition. Because the athletes only have a fixed time to make their lifts, our days never started earlier than 8 a.m., and never ended later than 5 p.m. Also, we were in an air-conditioned truck, so we avoided the crushing Atlanta heat.

The font entry person, Gerry Belec, and I had a heart-to-heart conversation before the first day of rehearsals. For a lot of people, the Olympics are a career stepping stone. It wasn't for me. I was already a producer, and I had no ambitions to be an event producer in sports. Gerry had advanced beyond entering numbers and letters. He worked the video board for Grateful Dead concerts. In fact, the crew he worked with would be producing the concerts at Centennial Park, the downtown entertainment hub for the Olympics. We agreed that we wanted to do a good job, but mostly we wanted to enjoy the experience. So, we planned to work hard during the rehearsals, get our systems nailed down during the first five days of competition, then party on the last five days.

The rehearsals were a disaster. This was the first Olympics where the system tabulating the official results was fed directly into the production truck, so we didn't have to enter the numbers manually. The system didn't work once during rehearsals. While the camera operators, switcher, and audio worked out any potential kinks, Gerry and I watched nervous IBM technicians sweat. They were still debugging the software on the first day of lifting, so Gerry had to type in a lot of names and numbers while I checked for accuracy.

Still, we were having a good time, going out at night, but not pushing it. IBM improved the systems every day, so our plan for the last five days was looking good. The night before our day off, the whole crew went to see George Clinton and the P-Funk All Stars at the House of Blues. We stayed out late, had a few drinks, and made the most of being able to sleep in the next day.

Gerry and I planned to spend most of the final five nights in the lighting and production towers at Centennial Park, watching concerts with his buddies from the Grateful Dead tours. But after the late night at the George Clinton concert, we decided to wait one more day to climb the tower. I watched TV and went to bed early.

The next morning, a phone call woke me up. It was my Uncle Carl. "Are you OK?"

"What? Yeah, why?"

"A bomb went off in Centennial Park last night."

"I'm OK. I was in my room last night. But thanks for checking on me."

I turned on the news to get the details. When I joined the crew for breakfast, no one was smiling. The sky was overcast, with some drizzling rain. When we arrived at the Georgia Dome, security felt like it was doubled. Police aircraft loomed overhead. The truck next to ours was deserted. It used to house the crew covering wrestling, but their event was over. Suddenly, it felt like we were reporting to prison, not work. A cameraman from LA said, "Let's get this over with and get the hell home."

Gerry had some news from his Grateful Dead friends. The explosion was at the base of the tower where we were going to watch the concerts. If the criminal had waited one more day, Gerry and I would have been standing on top of that bomb.

Members of our crew who had been to multiple Olympics said this was the worst one. That's probably true. Still, my Olympic experience is special to me. It helped that I'd added another baseball stadium to my collection before the games started.

I saw the Braves play the Florida Marlins at Atlanta-Fulton County Stadium, which opened in 1965, one of the first cookie cutter, multipurpose stadiums. It was round, like a hat box, non-descript, and completely lacking charm. The hat I bought, however, was revolutionary. It was the first I had purchased with the raised, or puff, stitching. The modification gave the hat some dimension, making the New Era 5950 even better, something I didn't think was possible. I like the italicized A, another simple, elegant logo. The dark blue hat with the bright red brim looks sharp too. This is a great hat.

Chicago White Sox
Style: structured, fitted
Made by New Era, 5950
Bought at the new Comiskey Park in Chicago in 1997

In 1996, Nancy came back to Toronto for another three-month work project. I invited her over to my place for dinner. After lasagna, before doing the dishes, while The Smashing Pumpkins' "Tonight, Tonight" played in the background, I kissed her. She must have liked it because we started dating. Still, I'd been through some long-distance relationships and knew how difficult they were to maintain, so I told her if she went back to Thunder Bay, there were no guarantees. Fortunately, her project was extended another three months. As that neared an end, I told her that if she was called back to Thunder Bay, we'd do our best to make it work. Her project was extended another three months. As that neared an end, I told her I didn't want her to go back.

The standard attractors were all there—her smile melted me, and she was smart as hell. I knew she would pass the dinner table test: the Colby family debates. Nancy could talk politics with the best of them, and was conversant on current events, religion, music, and movies. We enjoyed the same things, too. Saturday nights were spent at the Silver Dollar Room listening to blues bands that came through town. Nancy was equally at home at an opera or a baseball game. She had a glowing kindness that put people at ease but also a competitive fire that made her exciting. There was something else that elevated our relationship. It was like she looked inside me and saw who I was, not who she hoped I could be.

I could see her blossoming in the relationship, too. Already confident and competent, Nancy seemed lighter the longer we were together. We brought out the best in each other. There was none of the panging, dangerous edge of crazy love. Our bond was confident, natural. I think we were both realizing that we were better together than we ever could be apart. The deep connection I had always hoped for but wasn't sure existed was there. Our relationship was the mature partnership I had been looking for my entire romantic life. This was the higher love Steve Winwood sang about.

By early 1997, we started planning a vacation. I was going to Mexico to do some scuba diving in late July. Since we didn't know how much of the day diving would occupy, Nancy decided not to come. When I got back, we would go to Chicago, then home to Thunder Bay.

Nancy was on my mind the entire time I was in Mexico. I didn't want to be in a place like that without her again. We had never discussed marriage, but I decided I was going to propose to her.

When I got back, we spent a few days in Chicago, going to art museums, blues clubs, Wrigley Field, and to the New Comiskey Park to see the White Sox play the Blue Jays. That's where I bought this hat.

Just a note on New Comiskey. Unfortunately, it opened a year before Camden Yards in Baltimore, so it missed out on the old-looking-yet-new-feeling vibe of every stadium that came afterwards. The park is not great. It looks like they poured the concrete for the stands, bolted in the seats, and laid the sod on the field.

White Sox games had always been more workmanlike in contrast to the Cubs' north-side pretty-people party, and the new stadium only heightened that difference. On the plus side, it was an open air, natural grass ballpark, not a multipurpose stadium. There was another plus—the White Sox uniforms had undergone a major upgrade since my last visit to the south side, too. The dominant black color was a nod to the area's sooty industrial past. The stylish classic Sox on the hats and jerseys were a tribute to the team's long history. The White Sox felt like a more self-assured team in these uniforms.

At some point during the trip, I mentioned to Nancy that I was open to talking about a future together. Nancy said she didn't even want to consider it until she got a full-time job in Toronto. One was coming open in November. I decided not to mention marriage again, to anyone, until then.

On the way back from Chicago, we stopped in Alto, Michigan to visit my Great Uncle Bob, Great Aunt Marion, and my cousins. It was the first time they met Nancy, and she made quite an impression. After we left, Bob called my dad and said, "We have to do something, Pete. Craig can't let this girl get away."

I was about to find out how popular that opinion was.

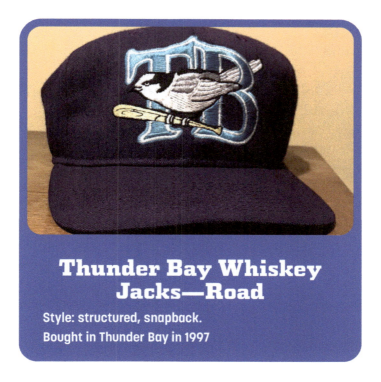

Thunder Bay Whiskey Jacks—Road

Style: structured, snapback.
Bought in Thunder Bay in 1997

After the trip to Chicago, and the stop in Michigan, Nancy and I went to Thunder Bay. My brother Jim and his children Danielle, five, and Mitch, three, would be there too. Danielle had visited me in Toronto earlier in the summer and spent some time with Nancy.

Her first question to Nancy was, "Do you live in a flat?" (Danielle lived in England at the time.)

Nancy said, "Yes."

"Do you live in *his* flat?"

"NO!"

In Thunder Bay, at a Whiskey Jacks game, Danielle sat between Nancy and me. Danielle looked at me and smiled, then looked at Nancy and smiled, then put her arms around both of us. Danielle's a Colby, so she didn't waste much time on subtlety. She'd waste even less on the ride home.

In the car, Danielle said in her sweetest voice, "Uncle Craig?"

"Yes, Dani?"

"I want a new aunt."

Nancy and I laughed uncomfortably. Then Danielle started to chant "I want a new aunt! I want a new aunt!"

Later in the trip, my parents threw a party at their house, with high school friends dropping over. I was in the kitchen when my dad cornered me. "Nancy is a really great woman. You'd better do right by her."

"OK," I replied.

I'd already decided to ask Nancy to marry me, but I couldn't do that for a few more months. I didn't want everyone to know about my intentions before Nancy did, so I wasn't going to encourage my dad's intervention.

Dad was determined though. "You need to marry her. You can't let her get away. Bob called me and said the same thing."

"All right, Dad. I'll take that into consideration."

That was not a satisfactory answer for Dad, so he pressed some more. Finally, I said, "I appreciate what you and Bob are saying, but this is my decision."

Dad replied, "Maybe so, but I'm still your father and I have a lot of influence over you."

Dad never talked this way. His MO was to watch, then ask questions. Rarely would he even give advice.

I replied, "Do you mean to say that if I thought I shouldn't marry someone, I'd do it just because you told me to?"

There was a pause. "No," he said.

"All right then. Thanks for the talk."

That ended the inquisition. However, a few nights later, he cornered me in the kitchen again and we had the same conversation.

It was nice to know so many people agreed. Nancy was the right woman for me.

Detroit Red Wings

Style: unstructured, strapback
Made by Fanatics
Bought in 2016 after the Red Wings qualified for the playoffs for the 25th straight year

After I moved to Toronto, the Red Wings started winning in a big way. Fortunately, working at TSN, I saw them play a lot. During the playoffs in 1989, the Red Wings' goalie consultant, Dave Dryden, sat beside me during the games.

The Wings became more than just a great hockey team. Their international roster was a United Nations of talent. The Russian Five—Sergei Fedorov, Vladimir Konstantinov, Slava Kozlov, Slava Fetisov, and Igor Larionov—were key parts of the Wings' first Stanley Cup win in 1997. When the captain, Steve Yzerman, handed the Cup to Fetisov and Larionov, Detroit showed the world the way it should be.

Watching Detroit's highly skilled, puck-possession game was like seeing a Degas painting spring to life while a poet reads you sonnets in the middle of a dinner of Kansas City ribs. They weren't just pretty, they were tough, too. A true Detroit team needs to be. In the midst of the Red Wings' ballet on ice, the Grind Line—Kris Draper, Kirk Maltby, Joe Kocur, and, later, Darren McCarty—banged like Keith Moon. Their shifts were sixty seconds of sweat and muscle.

The Red Wings did everything right. Steve Yzerman was named team captain when he was just twenty-one, a recognition that leadership transcends experience. When team owner Mike Ilitch learned that Rosa Parks, the mother of the civil rights movement, was assaulted and robbed in her Detroit apartment, he paid for her rent in a safer place to stay. Fans love their teams when they win, but this was something else. The Red Wings were an ideal that transcended borders and barriers.

On a personal note, I always loaded up on Red Wings in the company hockey playoff pool. When the Red Wings won the Cup in 1997, I won the pool. I'd been in Canada as an American for twenty-six years and claiming a victory in Canada's national game was the last push I needed to apply for my Canadian citizenship. So, in a way, the Red Wings made me international, too.

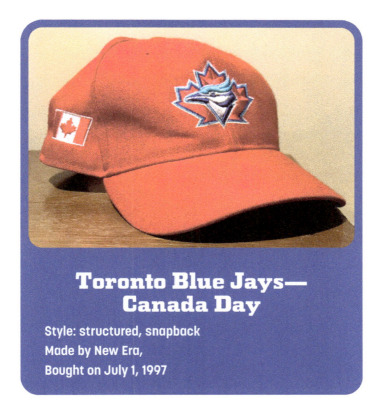

Toronto Blue Jays— Canada Day

Style: structured, snapback
Made by New Era,
Bought on July 1, 1997

Now that I had applied for my citizenship, I started thinking differently about Canada, Toronto, and even the Blue Jays.

In 1997, the American League and National League started playing regular-season games against each other for the first time. The Expos finally came to Toronto to play the Blue Jays in games that counted. I went to two of the three contests, including the Canada Day game. The Expos beat the Blue Jays 2-1. I cheered for the Expos since they were my National League team. It felt weird though. I lived in Toronto. Shouldn't I start cheering for the Jays when they weren't playing the Tigers?

Two things held me back. The first was the Jays' intense rivalry with the Tigers ten years earlier. Getting over the emotions from the Detroit-Toronto battles in the 1980s was hard. The second was the Blue Jays' home field, SkyDome, a terrible stadium. I called it the Anti-Septic Plastic Home Entertainment Dome. The field was artificial turf. It shared the concrete esthetics of the cookie-cutter, multipurpose stadiums from the 1960s.

I resented having to watch baseball here while other cities were building beautiful shrines to the game. Its only redeeming feature was the first functional, fully retractable roof in Major League Baseball, so you never had to miss a game because of bad weather. After weighing the Blue Jays' pros and cons, I bought this Canada Day Jays hat. We're supposed to root, root, root for the home team, right? It's in the song! This hat was part of the process of my becoming Canadian.

That process was finalized the next summer. I passed my citizenship test and Nancy joined me for the swearing-in ceremony at a government office in Scarborough, a suburb of Toronto. About twenty-five immigrants from around the world, a blend of shades, ages, and genders, sat well-dressed, waiting to officially belong. Friends and family were also there to share this big moment.

A short, fit clerk with a perfectly manicured beard burst into the room and made a beeline for the front desk. He raised his head and surveyed the crowd. Then he pointed to a person in the rear of the room. The clerk raised one finger and wagged it back and forth.

A confused silence replaced the joy in the room.

"You can't take pictures here," he said to a person holding a camera. "This is a legal affair. You can't take pictures in court. You can't take pictures here."

Then he delivered the orders we would have to follow if we wanted to become Canadian. "Pick up your papers here, then move on. Don't hesitate. It gets very congested."

Every Canadian knows this guy. He's the smallest player on the hockey team who spends the whole game hacking the bigger players and swearing at opponents from behind the ref. "You have to say the oath out loud! I'll be watching your lips!"

A man sitting next to me leaned over and whispered in an English accent, "Charming gentlemen."

Finally, the yippy clerk left, and the officiant came in. It was Roy Bonisteel, a prominent Canadian journalist and host for the CBC. His hair was white and his smile broad. Bonisteel was warm and welcoming, but his sunshine had already been eclipsed by the jerk who preceded him.

I received my citizenship papers, but Nancy was appalled. She was ready to start writing letters. I wanted to talk to the clerk afterward, but in true weasel fashion, he was long gone before he would have to face any consequences for his rudeness. Despite the bad day, becoming Canadian was an overwhelmingly good thing. I was now a citizen of two countries. The border no longer applied to me.

Team Colby

Style: structured, fitted
Custom hat

In November 1997, Nancy landed the full-time job in Toronto she had applied for. The next day I got a loan and bought an engagement ring.

I told Nancy we should exchange our Christmas gifts alone before we went to Thunder Bay for the holidays. On December 19, 1997, I picked her up at the apartment she was sharing with her friend Laura, who had moved home to Toronto.

I didn't tell Nancy where we were going. We parked downtown and started walking toward SkyDome. "Not Planet Hollywood!" Nancy exclaimed as we approached the celebrity-worshipping cesspool masquerading as a restaurant.

We blew past that odious goo palace, and walked to the bottom of the CN Tower, the tallest freestanding structure in Toronto and, for a time, the world. An express elevator took us to the 360, a restaurant above the observation level. It's an upscale place with excellent food. Our seats were by the window. The night was clear and the city where we met glistened below us, like it knew what was coming. We held hands and had an amazing dinner. Then we exchanged gifts. I gave her a watch. She gave me a sweet Detroit Lions Barry Sanders road jersey that I'd love to show you, but this is a book about hats.

Nancy said, "This is perfect"—referring to the evening, not the jersey.

Knowing I was about to change my life filled me with an odd self-awareness. I felt detached and present at the same time.

I reached down into a gift bag below the table and held the ring box in my sweaty palm.

"Nancy, I have a really good life. I know it will be a happy one."

Then I lifted the white ring box and pulled open the lid, revealing a single diamond framed by dual crescendos of a gold band. The ring was elegant, understated, and beautiful—like the woman in the maroon crushed-velvet dress sitting across from me.

Nancy's hands went to her face. Her eyes filled with tears. We had never had a serious discussion about marriage.

"But to be truly happy, I need you in my life."

I removed the ring from the box, took Nancy's left hand, and started to put the ring on her trembling finger. Suddenly, I realized I hadn't asked the question yet. I pulled the ring back.

"Nancy, will you marry me?"

The answer came in a gasp. "Yes."

I pushed the ring onto her finger. Then we rushed around the table and kissed, holding each other for a long time.

It was official. Nancy agreed with my dad, Danielle, and my great uncle Bob, too. We belonged together.

After dinner, we went to the observation level. The glass floor scares the hell out of me. When I look down at what appears to be a certain plunge to my death, my body stiffens like a board. Nancy and I approached the terrifying, transparent panes, held hands, and walked across it, together.

The next day, we shared the news. My nephew Mitch, four, would be the ring bearer, my niece Danielle, six, the flower girl. Danielle immediately asked, "What are your colors?" When we told Mitch we wanted him to help with the wedding, he cheerfully said, "I can help with the wedding! I can build a wall in the church! Then I'll paint the wall!" We told him the job would be a little easier than that.

Nancy chose her friends Laura Boast and Lisa MacGillivray as bridesmaids and her sister Mary Ellen as her maid-of-honor. My brothers Jim and Scott would be my groomsmen and Dave my best man.

Dave was a natural. He was married for seven years and had two boys, Ryan, three, and Ben, one, at the time of the wedding. On August 1, 1998, a few weeks after I became a Canadian citizen, I waited for the ceremony to begin in the rectory at a church in Thunder Bay with my brothers and Dave. Dave said, "When you see Nancy at the back of the church in her dress, you're going to cry."

"Really?" The thought hadn't occurred to me.

Sure enough, when Nancy walked through the back doors and I saw her in the veil and white gown, tears came to my eyes. Dave called it. The ceremony was an efficient half hour. Dave Stiff said it was timed like a TV show. As we walked down the aisle, I saw the faces of so many people we both loved smiling back at us.

We took some wedding party pictures, then went to Boston Pizza for a bite and drink before the reception.

Dave's speech was hilarious, and not much about me or Nancy. Instead, he skewered my entire family. "If you're in a conversation with the Colbys and don't have an opinion about the topic, don't worry. One will be assigned to you."

The reception was a blast. Some little girls asked Danielle if she was a princess. When "Baby Don't Hurt Me" came on, my friends bounced Nancy between them like they were Will Ferrell in that "Saturday Night Live" skit. Nancy said all she could see was John Petrynka's big red shirt coming right at her. The DJ played "Soul Man" while Dave and I recreated our Blues Brothers dance moves

After the last song, "Stairway to Heaven," a nod to our high school dances, Nancy and I retired to our room with a hot tub.

The next morning at breakfast, we saw Relita with Ryan and Ben. I asked where Dave was and Ryan replied, "Dad has the flu." It could have been worse. Relita told me that when Dave tried to have a nap on the bench in front of the venue, a couple of guys tried to roll him for his wallet. His mother Sue had to chase them away.

The ceremony and reception were all I could have hoped for. I had these hats made for my wedding party and for Nancy. Of course, they were Detroit Tigers' colors.

Two days after the wedding, Nancy and I got out of dodge and went on our honeymoon. The best part of my life was about to begin.

Oakland Athletics—Home
Style: Structured, fitted
Made by New Era, 5950
Bought in San Francisco in 1998 on my honeymoon

I knew I'd married well when my bride agreed to spend the first night of her honeymoon at a baseball game in Oakland.

Nancy picked San Francisco as our honeymoon destination. I picked a few baseball games as activities. We landed in San Francisco, rented a convertible, and drove to Oakland.

The Oakland A's stadium—Oakland Alameda County Coliseum—was a dump. It was a multipurpose, concrete blah. Because the seating set-up is so round to accommodate football, the foul territory is ridiculously large, putting the fans farther away from the action and creating an unfair advantage for pitchers. Popups that would land in the stands in other places landed in fielders' gloves here. At least it had real grass.

Despite playing in an old stadium, in a small market, the A's are frequently competitive. Oakland was one of the pioneers of the analytic approach to baseball, breaking down the numbers to assess players, as documented in the book "Moneyball," and as dramatized in the movie of the same name.

Their green and gold uniforms always look fantastic, whether in the crazy pajama style of the 1970s championship teams, or the more refined style they've worn since the late 1980s. This is my favorite version of their cap. The dark green contrasts well with the vibrant yellow. I like the stylized A with the superfluous possessive apostrophe (isn't Athletics plural? Are we to believe this hat belongs to the team?).

The A's look good and play well. They're the smart kid, with great style from a poor neighborhood. They leave their unkempt rental home in the morning in sharp vintage thrift-shop clothes on their way to ace an exam, then go to work at a minimum-wage job. They don't have the advantages other teams enjoy, but the Athletics don't let that stop them.

I'd ordered seats in the upper deck behind home plate. Our tickets included a free buffet. We arrived late and the line for food was long. Meanwhile, the New York Yankees were teeing off on A's starter Mike Oquist like it was batting practice. We were missing the action and I was getting antsy.

Nancy said, "I just want a hot dog." So, we bought a couple of hot dogs and took our seats, wearing our wedding hats.

It wasn't much of a game. The Yankees scored one run in the first inning, seven in the second and five in the third on their way to a 14-1 win. Oquist pitched five innings and gave up all fourteen runs. The manager left him in because there was a doubleheader the next day and the A's didn't want to burn out their pitching staff. Talk about taking one for the team. Oquist was as beat up as the ballpark.

I couldn't find a hat at the stadium (what the hell, Oakland!), but picked one up later in the trip. It had been there a while because the stitching wasn't raised, the new style. That was a letdown. However, the first night of our honeymoon was glorious. The game may have been a blowout and the stadium shabby, but my new wife was luminous, smiling and laughing in the summer air. I still couldn't believe I was lucky enough to spend my life with her.

San Francisco Giants
Style: structured, fitted
Made by New Era, 5950
Bought at Candlestick Park in 1998

I swear we didn't spend our entire honeymoon at the ballpark. After our night in Oakland, we explored San Francisco. We happened to go to Alcatraz on the one day each year former inmates, guards and their families gather to tell their stories. The guards who lived on the island with their families felt so safe, they didn't lock their doors. We also saw the movie "Saving Private Ryan." So, on our honeymoon, Nancy and I went to a brutal war movie and a prison. The baseball games look pretty good now, don't they?

We also went to Napa to visit wineries for a day then drove down the California coast to Monterey. The temperature dropped by about fifty degrees Fahrenheit. We kept the top down on the convertible as long as we could stand the cold wind. We stopped at the legendary Pebble Beach Golf Club to have a look around. As we walked back to our car, Don Johnson and Cheech Marin pulled up in a Porsche and took out their golf clubs.

I looked over at my wife. Nancy was standing about six feet from the Hollywood stars and, thanks to our long drive with the top down, her hair looked like it belonged on a bride—the bride of Frankenstein. Not the brush with fame she would have liked.

Near the end of the trip, we saw the San Francisco Giants play the Braves at the fabled, and crappy, Candlestick Park. The Stick was another multipurpose mess devoid of character. It had a reputation for being cold all the time. The game started at 5 p.m. Our upper deck, first-base seats were in the sun when the game started, so it was nice. When night descended, it was freezing, even for a couple of Canadians.

I was excited to see the Giants. They'd relocated from New York to California for the 1958 season—along with the Dodgers, who moved from Brooklyn to Los Angeles the same year. But the Giants' move is always treated as a historical afterthought. The Dodgers seemed to have more personality, both in Brooklyn and Los Angeles.

The Giants didn't look they cared about that. They looked tough and confident, with their uniforms emphasizing black over orange. Their cold, spartan stadium only added to the impression. In the 1990s, their surly star Barry Bonds did, too.

At the game we attended, Bonds homered twice, but the Braves broke a 5-5 tie with two runs in the ninth to win, 7-5. Great game. Two teenage girls sitting behind us saw "bride" and "groom" stitched on the back of our wedding hats and said "Congratulations!" The lids paid off. Nancy called the game one of the highlights of the trip.

I love this Giants hat. The interlocking block orange SF on the black background looks bold and secure. I wore this Giants hat a lot until San Francisco swept Detroit in the 2012 World Series. I was at Game Four. It still stings.

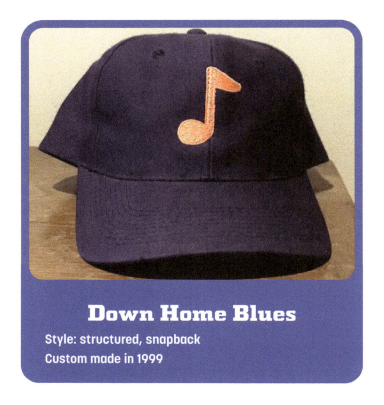

Down Home Blues
Style: structured, snapback
Custom made in 1999

In Toronto, I played mixed slo-pitch with teams from work. We won a few championships in the media league, but it wasn't very competitive. So, I joined the Willowdale Slo-pitch league in North York, the Toronto suburb where Nancy and I lived, playing for the local Valu-mart supermarket. I didn't know anyone in the league, but I had a good time. We won the championship and I won Most Sportsmanlike Player.

As the league expanded, I was asked to captain a team. This wasn't a surprise. I was never the best, but in high school I won all the leadership awards. I was the captain of the football and soccer team, won the Rotary Citizenship Award, was voted valedictorian, and was given an award for student leadership by the Thunder Bay Board of Education. In university, I was a resident assistant, in charge of a floor in a residence. Putting together and running the team would be a breeze. Fun, too.

I immediately abused my authority, arbitrarily assigning us Detroit Tigers colors and naming the team the Down Home Blues, after the classic blues song by ZZ Hill. I didn't ask anyone else's opinion. I just did it. Nancy played, along with a lot of TSN and Discovery friends.

I established two team rules. First, let me know if you can't make it to a game. Second, don't act like a jerk. You can be a jerk, just don't act like one at the games. If you broke rule number one often enough, you had broken rule number two. The Blues played smart and hard, but we also understood this was Sunday night rec league softball. We were there to have fun, not create more stress in our lives. In our first year, we won the championship. I caught the final out. We were in the finals six straight seasons, winning three championships with one tie (don't get me started on that one).

As life got busier, this is where I saw my friends. Over the years, our roster was made up of a lot of couples and siblings. The team was together for twenty-one seasons until the pandemic shut us down for a year.

The first version of the hat is a pedestrian structured snapback, but later versions were much better. The second was an unstructured strapback with an orange underbrim and the latest is a structured New Era snapback with raised stitching on the orange note. I adhered to the principles of a good baseball hat: a simple logo with limited colors. Gorgeous.

Detroit Tigers
Style: unstructured, strapback
Made by Twins Enterprise, which later became '47 Brand

The last year of the twentieth century was also the last year for Tiger Stadium, my favorite place on Earth. Some of the happiest days of my life were spent in the stands, draped in Tigers' gear, watching the team play. Day games felt warm and tranquil. Night games buzzed with excitement as the light towers fought off the darkness, allowing the ballet of baseball to play out on grass and dirt.

Of course, no sporting event would ever be better than watching the Tigers win the division in 1987, or seeing the Tigers win Game Four of the World Series in 1984. But my love for this place outstripped any handful of games. I liked sports in high school, but I learned to love them in university by crossing the river and feeling them in person.

I had been to more Tigers game than any other team. In these blue and orange seats, I had learned the elegant shorthand of recording the games from the Tiger Stadium scorecards. Bonds were formed, not just to the team, but with people sitting next to me.

Susan and I had studied in between innings here before exams. Dave taunted me when the Orioles' Mike Young hit a grand slam into the upper deck in rightfield off Tigers' relief pitcher Aurelio Lopez, Senior Smoke, to give Baltimore the win. "Senior Upper Deck," Dave gloated. In 1984, Scott and I had spent his birthday in the leftfield grandstand, watching the Tigers beat the Blue Jays. The next night we sat in the rain in the upper-deck bleachers, cheering at Tigers' centerfielder Chet Lemon until he waved at us.

In 1986, the day before I graduated from university, my parents joined my brother Jim, his girlfriend Lynn, Susan, and me in infield seats to see the Tigers beat the Jays; it was just a week before Susan and I broke up. A few months later, Missy and I watched the Tigers battle the Yankees from first-base seats in the lower deck. In 1988, a friend of Scott's showed us how to pay off the umpires to get a seat right behind home plate. In 1989, Scott and I sat in the upper deck on the third-base side and watched a lunar eclipse appear over the first-base side facade.

When Nancy and I started dating, I brought her to a game against Cleveland. To really understand me, I thought she needed to feel the corner of Michigan and Trumball's aura. If I loved someone, I brought them to Tiger Stadium.

In my single days, my passion for the place mingled with some more obvious desires. I'd had a fantasy about the Tiger Stadium infield, "Born to Run" playing on the stadium speakers, and a prominent Canadian figure skater. That was never going to happen, although I know two people who later dated her, so maybe it was just bad timing. Yeah, that's probably it.

But the stadium had lived its full life. The concrete was crumbling, and the times demanded modern conveniences, for both the fans, now accustomed to wide concourses, unobstructed views, and luxury boxes, and the players, who had long complained about the cramped quarters in the locker rooms. Knowing the closure made perfect sense made it no less painful to say goodbye. My farewell would be this night.

Dave and I arrived at our final game at baseball heaven with a noble quest—to get some dirt from the field. Our seats were in the first row between the dugout and third base. We waved plastic cups at the grounds crew, but they ignored our pleas. They were busy anyway. It was a misty night, and the tarp was still on the infield. It looked like we were out of luck.

I settled in with a beer, a hot dog, my scorecard, and a pencil to enjoy my last night ever at Tiger Stadium.

Just before game time, the crew rolled up the tarp, and stored it right in front of our seats. Dave and I looked at each other. The tarp was covered in wet infield dirt. Dave pulled plastic bags out of his pocket, and I scooped dirt off the tarp with my scorecard. Mission accomplished.

Then we watched the Tigers give up ten runs in the seventh in a 12-6 loss to the Blue Jays. It hurt so much. Somehow, losing to Toronto, the Tigers archrival from the mid-'80s and a team I had grudgingly agreed to cheer for when they weren't playing Detroit, made it even worse. But at least we had a small piece of Tiger Stadium to take home with us.

I adore this hat. The muted navy fabric, ragged Tigers logo patch, and Detroit pennant on the side gives the hat a subdued nostalgia. This cap recalls the team's rich history, especially my happy times in the gorgeous confines of Tiger Stadium.

Milwaukee County Stadium
Style: structured, snapback
It was a giveaway in 1999

Dave decided we needed to see Milwaukee County Stadium, which was also in its final season in 1999. Well, it was supposed to be its final season. We planned a trip with our friends Dave Mack, Phillip Whalley, John Petrynka, and Paul Manary.

Dave Mack and I played football together. After high school, Dave Mack bought into the ownership of the Thunder Bay Truck Centre, a reflection of his business ambitions and leadership. Dave Mack was athletic, principled, and not reluctant to share his point of view. Phil and I went way back. I met him in Grade 3 when I moved to Thunder Bay. He was an avid outdoorsman. In high school, Phil was named Best Conversationalist for his proficient profanity. Calling Phil forthcoming was like calling a heat-seeking missile direct. Phil was also thoughtful, so his words carried a double impact. He became an electrician at Hydro One.

John Petrynka was unfailingly good natured, with an easy smile and a soft tone, not a combination you always find in a drummer. Because he took a joke so well, he was frequently at their receiving end. JP worked in auto parts.

Paul was the only one who didn't go to high school with us. We met him at our Sunday baseball games, where his pal Tim Cattani told us his name was Roger, as a joke. Paul enjoyed the joke so much that he didn't correct people. I stumbled on the truth, but it took years. I kept calling him Roger anyway. When we formed the O'Tooles softball team, Dave had trouble locating Paul. "I keep calling that number, but they say Roger doesn't live there," Dave explained. "That's because his name is actually Paul," I replied. "Oh," Dave said. No one had let him in on the joke. Paul was now a pharmacist. He had an impish grin and ready laugh.

On the first night, we stayed in Madison, Wisconsin. Even one day into the trip, the vibe was different than the earlier baseball trips Dave and I had taken. We were all older, married, some with children. Most of us were leaders at work, in charge of teams if not companies. All of us were more accustomed to having our opinions accepted.

That doesn't work with old friends. We all seemed to bristle when our wisdom was countered. That night in the hotel, Dave Mack and I got into a full argument, broken only when Dave Mack said something that pissed off Phil, who came charging in.

The tension lingered for a little while, but the relationships weren't affected. I think we all needed it. I sure did. Your friends are there to tell you when you're full of it, and all of us were, to varying degrees. As Irish writer Oscar Wilde said, "Your true friends stab you in the front." By breakfast, everyone was happy and ready for the next leg.

Somewhere on the drive, we stopped at a gas station to fuel up and get snacks. Dave Hagberg pointed to a bag of Combos, pretzels stuffed with cheese, and said that his son Ryan hated those snacks. The Hagbergs took unusual pride in things like that. Dave had never seen "Star Wars." His mother Sue had never been inside a convenience store. Ryan was making his stand on Combos.

When Dave wasn't looking, I bought a bag of Combos and snuck them into the van. I hopped into the front passenger seat, Dave sat in the seat behind me, Dave Mack hopped in front to take his turn driving. I pulled out the bag of Combos.

"Combos!" Dave Mack exclaimed. "I love Combos! I don't like sweet snacks, but I love salty ones. These are perfect!" I looked back at Dave Hagberg, who was stifling a laugh. I told Dave Mack, "They're all yours." Dave Mack guided us to our destination, happily munching on Ryan Hagberg's most hated food.

Later that afternoon, we arrived in Milwaukee, where we picked up the inaccurate giveaway hats. They were inaccurate because the week before, a crane that was being used to build the replacement stadium collapsed, killing three people. The damage was so bad, County Stadium would be used for one more year.

The park was definitely a throwback. County Stadium opened in 1953. It felt like a big minor league park, charming and intimate. I liked to think of Hank Aaron playing there.

The Brewers seem like a little brother to me. They arrived in Milwaukee in 1970 after going bankrupt in their one season as the Seattle Pilots. Milwaukee's previous team, the Braves, had moved to Atlanta for the 1966 season, which must have broken hearts.

So, the Brewers started as a replacement both for the Braves and the Pilots. The Brew Crew had some terrific teams in the 1980s but lost their only World Series appearance to the St. Louis Cardinals in seven games in 1982.

The city had a great baseball tradition, but the team's uniforms seemed neither new nor classic—rather torn between the two. Bright blue and yellow suggest the new, but their pinstripes represent the tradition. When we saw them, the Brewers were going for a more traditional look, using a darker blue and gold but without pinstripes. It wasn't an improvement.

We had seats in the lower deck on the third-base side, right beside a pillar. Dave took a walk and came back with some County Stadium dirt. I have no idea how he got it. Dave looked right at home in Milwaukee. He had the same build as a lot of the fans. The men here clearly worked out and drank beer, with broad shoulders and a strong frame over a thick middle. The stadium looked like it was full of Daves.

Our next stop was Wrigley Field. Dave and I had been there, but our friends hadn't, and they needed to feel the magic. We had ordered tickets from the club, but none of the seats was together. That wouldn't do. A scalper outside the stadium swapped our seats for bleacher tickets. Then we all bought Cubs hats.

When the gates opened, we were the first ones in, claiming bench spots in leftfield. Some guy in front of us was wearing a shirt that said "Rightfield Sucks" on the back. That tells you a lot about human nature.

Dave Mack and I went to buy beer for the group. Most stadiums had a beer limit per customer to tamper rowdiness. At the concession stand, we asked how many beers we could have. The vendor looked at us blankly, "How many can you carry?"

We could carry a lot.

Before the game, Cubs first baseman Mark Grace walked out to the bleachers and threw a ball into the stands. Then he called for it back. For the next ten minutes, he played catch with the fans.

The guys sitting next to us started a game with a cup. Everyone put a dollar in, then one person held the cup for an at-bat. If the batter got a hit, you took out a dollar. If he hit a double, you took out two, and three for a triple. If the batter hit a home run, the person holding the cup got all the money. If the batter was out, you put in another dollar and passed the cup. I was invited to join the game. I don't remember if the cup game lasted the duration of the baseball game. I lost track of the baseball game altogether. You can't blame me. We were in the Wrigley Field Bleachers. And we could carry a lot of beer.

The Cubs won. Or lost. I don't remember. Does it matter? My pals and I had a great time in an A+ baseball environment. We all understood the cohesion between friends who had seen each other at our best and worst, sometimes in the same weekend, and appreciated both. Strong friendships are bound by willing vulnerability. To this day, in each of our houses, there is a framed picture of the six of us in the Wrigley Field bleachers in our Cubs caps. It was one of the best days of my life.

There's a footnote to this story. Years later, I mailed Dave Mack a gift in a small bubble-wrap package. It arrived while he was away on business. Dave's wife and three daughters were intrigued. What could Craig have sent? The package sat on a counter all week, the hidden contents tormenting them. When Dave walked in the door at the end of the week, the four women immediately handed him the package, demanding that he end the suspense. Dave ripped open the seal and pulled out a package of Combos with a Post-It note saying, "I thought you'd enjoy these." Renee, Dave Mack's oldest daughter, didn't hide her disappointment. "Your friends are all weird, Dad," she declared, as they all stomped off.

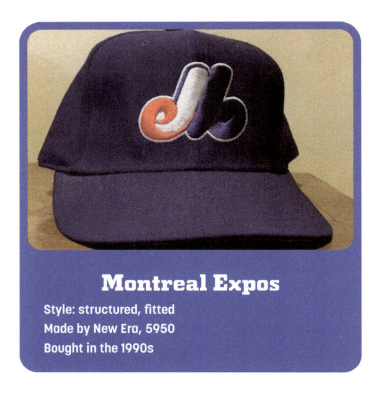

Montreal Expos
Style: structured, fitted
Made by New Era, 5950
Bought in the 1990s

The Expos original tri-color hats were unique, like the team. They were the first MLB team outside of the US and they played in a weird stadium. Olympic Stadium looked like a concrete flying saucer with a periscope. Their change to a more traditional uniform in the 1990s was a mistake. If you're weird, then weird it up, man!

In 1999, Nancy and I went to see the Expos play the Houston Astros with Nancy's bridesmaid Lisa MacGillivray. Our Montreal-based friends Marc Stevens and his wife Marianne joined us. Marianne worked with me at Discovery Channel, but I really hit it off with Marc, a sports fan and blues enthusiast.

Olympic Stadium was built for the 1976 Summer Games. It had a big plastic tarp roof that was retractable until it broke. Watching baseball here was like being in a bunker under a giant umbrella, hardly in keeping with the game's pastoral romance. It was far from the most beautiful place to spend a summer evening. Montreal fans had also been burned by the 1994 strike. The Expos had the best record in baseball when the games stopped. Over the next few seasons, the owners dismantled the team to save money. The combination of heartbreak at missing the team's best chance at a World Series, anger with the owners, and having to watch baseball in a Tupperware cave kept fans away. Just 8,471 fans were with us to see the Expos lose 5-2 to the Houston Astros but the crowd sounded bigger. In key moments, people banged the empty seats up and down. It made a hellacious noise!

Because I'm such a baseball hat freak, I bought one of these bland Expos hats before we went to Montreal even though I didn't like it very much. What I remember most from the game is that Nancy put her overnight bag on top of my Expos hat in the back seat of the car. I discovered the infraction in the parking lot before the game. Fortunately, the hat popped back into shape after I rescued it. Somehow, our marriage survived.

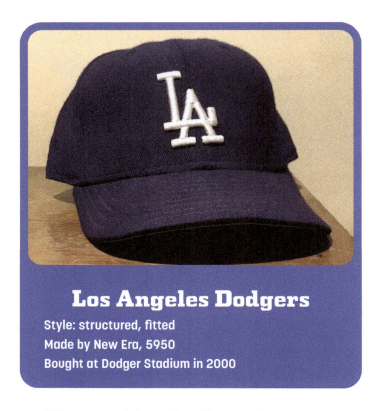

Los Angeles Dodgers
Style: structured, fitted
Made by New Era, 5950
Bought at Dodger Stadium in 2000

When my Discovery Channel colleague Sam Linton got pregnant after producing the highest-rated series in the channel's history, Season 1 of "The Sex Files," management asked me to take over.

It was a step up, so I negotiated a big raise. They came in at the low end of the range I'd suggested but would give me a bonus that would get me to the top end if I beat the previous year's numbers. No easy task.

I had three goals. The first was to get that bonus. The second was to make the best television series ever. The third was to manipulate the production schedule so I could see both of Bruce Springsteen's concerts in Toronto and go to a Dodgers game in Los Angeles.

I nailed the last goal right away. After back-to-back Boss shows, I spent three weeks traveling all over North America and Europe. On the last leg, I flew from Copenhagen to Toronto on a Sunday, dropped off shoot tapes, picked up new ones, did laundry, kissed my wife, then flew to Los Angeles Monday morning. When I arrived, I was still feeling the nine-hour time change.

The Dodgers were playing the Reds, but only that night. It was my sole chance to go to Dodger Stadium. I thought, *What's the big deal? It's a three-hour game. I'll be back in the hotel by 10:30 and get eight hours of sleep before the crew call.*

I rented a Jeep across the street from our Santa Monica hotel and drove to Chavez Ravine. The parking lot was almost empty. As soon as I pulled up, a guy offered me a ticket a few rows behind third base at face value. The Lakers were playing Portland in the NBA semi-finals that night. This early season Dodgers game was an afterthought for LA sports fans.

I bought the ticket and, once inside the stadium, immediately bought this hat. I didn't know it at the time, but the crown tilts away from the brim. It bugs me because I love the Dodgers' classic lid. The interlocking LA is a brilliant design—clear, simple, and elegant. The white stitching on the royal blue background perfectly reflects the Dodgers' identity, bright and sunny.

This was a team of stars in a land of stars. Their uniforms—royal script over white at home and gray on the road with red numbers—are perfect, a classic look with a little bit of understated "Look at me." The Dodgers know who they are. However, because of the odd fit of this particular cap, I don't wear it much.

Dodger Stadium is set into a ravine. The entrance is at the top of the stadium. From there, I descended into the lower decks. Dodger Stadium was built in the 1960s, but it doesn't feel outdated. You can see trees and rolling hills over the outfield wall. It's a lovely place to watch a game.

The guy next to me was a Mexican gentleman who didn't speak much English. I loved the way he said, "Go Doyers." I now call the Dodgers "Doyers" about 50 percent of the time. My new friend bought me a beer, which I was trying to avoid because I was still jet lagged. I had to return the favor. After two beers, I was sleepy but kept my eyes open. It couldn't be too bad, right? I'd only be here for three hours.

The game went fourteen innings, lasted four and a half hours, and ended on what should have been an easy force-out at home, except that the Reds' catcher, Ed Taubensee, took his foot off the plate before he had the ball. I guess he was tired, too. The Dodgers won a weird one. I left exhausted. At a red light on my way to the hotel, I fell asleep at the wheel. I woke up with the car idling, the light green, and, fortunately, no one else around. About ten minutes later I was back at the hotel, exhausted, but unscathed.

By the way, I accomplished my first goal, too. "The Sex Files" Season Two increased its ratings over Season One by thirty percent, becoming the highest-rated series in the channel's history at the time. The season premiere was the highest-rated Canadian single program on the channel, and the fifth-highest-rated program of any kind. It made my career.

As for goal number two, was it the best television series ever? That's subjective, but let's just say yes.

New York Mets
Style: structured, fitted
Made by New Era, 5950
Bought at Shea Stadium in 2000

In 2000, Nancy and I took a vacation to New York City. We saw a David Letterman show, "Aida" by Elton John and Tim Rice on Broadway, and went to a Mets game with my brother Jim, his wife Lynn and their kids—my niece Danielle, nine, and nephew Mitch, seven. Shea Stadium looked like an Erector Set with the inner structure exposed. The walkways to the upper deck were in the open air, making the stadium look like it was made of wobbly pancakes. The place felt unfinished. I'm pretty sure even Mets fans didn't love it, but Mets fans are used to compromise. The team was built on it.

The Mets started play in 1962, a one-team replacement for the two that had left: the Dodgers to Los Angeles and the Giants to San Francisco. Their colors were a melding of the Dodgers' blue and Giants' orange.

The Mets are a sharp contrast to the iconic Yankees. By playing out in Queens, they feel more like a neighborhood team. Mets fans embraced their patchwork beginnings and lower profile with classic New York defiance. Their hats have a beautiful, stylized interlocking NY, and they wore pinstripes even as an expansion team. We've got your tradition right here! Unfortunately, when I saw the Mets, they had adopted black as a primary color. It felt like a mid-life crisis, changing their clothes to look tough and cool. The Mets didn't need it. They had already established themselves as both in their hardscrabble existence.

Nancy, Mitch, Danielle, and I were all wearing Mets hats. It pays to gear up. We were sitting in the upper deck on the first-base side when the mascot, Mr. Met, showed up with a pizza and a surprise. We'd been upgraded to lower deck seats behind first base.

We had to abandon Jim and Lynn, who were not wearing Mets hats. Fortunately, there were empty seats around us, so I went back to the upper deck to get Jim and Lynn and they snuck into our new section.

When the Mets hit a home run, a big apple pops up beyond the outfield wall. Mitch really wanted to see it. The Mets were beating the Pittsburgh Pirates 8-0 late in the game but hadn't hit a home run. It looked like Mitch was going to leave disappointed. In the bottom of the eighth, Melvin Mora finally popped one out. The big apple made its appearance. Mitch was so happy. It's funny how much those extra flourishes make a difference.

That was a great day at the ballpark. Also, I love the Mets caps.

Detroit Tigers—
Style: structured, fitted
Made by American Needle
Bought in the 2000s

The Tigers' new home, Comerica Park, opened in 2000. Naturally, Dave and I drove down for a game. The Tigers beat the A's 4-3. It was disorienting to see the Tigers play a home game in a different stadium, especially one so . . . different.

Tiger Stadium was a hitter's park, with seating all the way around the upper deck outfield. Comerica Park was a huge pitcher's park. The field was so big, the players called it Comerica National Park. Watching the Tigers here felt like I was cheating on Tiger Stadium.

However, the new stadium was gorgeous. The concourses were open, so you could see game play from everywhere. Pillars featuring Tigers' history were all over the place. A Tigers merry-go-round and a baseball Ferris wheel were included for the kids. Centerfield opened to show the best of

Detroit's skyline, the gleaming towers of the Renaissance Center, and the old brick buildings closer to the stadium.

Well done! The Tigers created a new home that celebrated the team's legacy.

This gorgeous retro hat does the same thing. It's from the Cooperstown Collection, made by Major League Baseball to celebrate the history of the game. The cap puts an old design on a modern hat structure. I love it.

Pittsburgh Pirates—Home
Style: structured, fitted
Made by New Era, 5950
Bought at PNC Park in 2001

In the summer of 2001, Dave came to Toronto and joined me and my colleagues Larry and Chris Tapanila on another baseball road trip. We were going to see the Yankees and Tigers in Detroit, and then catch some games in Pittsburgh.

The Steel City wasn't what I expected. Beautiful forests along the highway suddenly open to reveal the confluence of the Three Rivers—Allegheny, Monongahela, and Ohio—sheltered by the big shoulders of the surrounding hills. Train trestles span the rivers. In the heart of it is a jewel of a city bursting with stunning architecture. This is no dirty little town.

I was excited to see the Pirates play. The team was formed in the late 1800s. Like the city, the Pirates had seen good times and bad. The Buccos had won five World Series, the last in 1979 with a team appropriate for the age. The disco-era Pirates played in a concrete multipurpose stadium, wore a variety of garish outfits, and adopted the dance hit "We Are Family" by Sister Sledge as their anthem.

At the dawn of the twenty-first century, the Pirates wore uniforms more fitting with their history. The black and gold colors are perfect for the soot and molten metal industry that built the city. The block P looks strong. This is a weathered team that endures. Their stadium also felt more in keeping with this solid, beautiful place.

PNC Park is gorgeous—black steel and tan limestone with a beautiful view of the city, especially on the third base side where you see yellow bridges spanning the river. Restaurants are built into the outside of the stadium. We had a great Italian meal before the game.

The rightfield wall is twenty-one feet, a tribute to Pirates legend Roberto Clemente. He died in a plane crash December 31, 1972, while on his way to help with earthquake relief in Nicaragua. The Hall of Fame waived the five-year waiting period before induction and Clemente was elected in 1973. This is one of my favorite places to watch baseball. Stunning.

I don't remember much about the game except that the Phillies pounded the Pirates and there were so many substitutions it made a mess of my scorecard. Also, the Pirate mascot bit Dave on the head. Then we went back to the hotel, shot pool, and drank Iron City Lager.

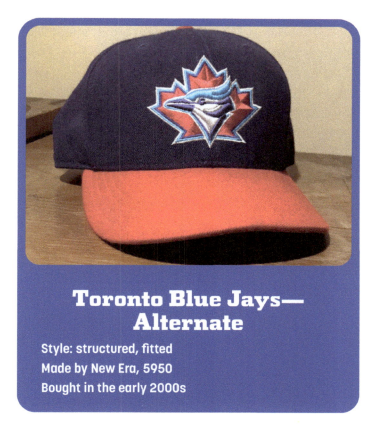

Toronto Blue Jays— Alternate

Style: structured, fitted
Made by New Era, 5950
Bought in the early 2000s

I'm not sure exactly when I broke down and bought this cap. I like the red brim and the big maple leaf. It's a little busy, with one color too many, but the Jays are a non-traditional team, so they get some leeway. Despite committing to cheering for the home team when they weren't playing the Tigers, of course, it still felt weird to own a Blue Jays cap, let alone to wear it. Nice hat though. It really shows New Era's amazing stitching.

New Era was born in 1920. Ehrhardt Koch, a German immigrant, borrowed money from his sister to start a hat company. They opened a shop in a back room in Buffalo. In 1934, they started making hats for Cleveland's baseball team. By 1950, they'd added the Brooklyn Dodgers, Cincinnati

Reds, and Detroit Tigers (Go Tigers) as clients. In 1954, they created their masterpiece, the 5950.

In 1980, they started selling the official hats to fans through "The Sporting News." Of course, hard-core fans wanted an official hat! I bought my first 5950 four years later at Sportsland USA, across from Tiger Stadium. It changed me.

Hats transformed from utilitarian sun blockers into art you wear. In the 1990s, New Era became the official supplier to all Major League Baseball teams. A few years later, filmmaker Spike Lee, a massive Yankees fan, talked them into making a red New York Yankees cap, giving birth to the fashion cap. That's when I started seeing the hat I loved everywhere, not just on the heads of hardcore sports lovers. The 5950 no longer belonged to just baseball fanatics.

Ottawa Lynx

Style: structured, fitted
Made by New Era, 5950
Bought in Ottawa in 2001.

Nancy and I saw the Expos' Triple A farm team, the Lynx, when we visited our friend Lisa MacGillivray in Ottawa in 2001. Minor league baseball is wonderful. The tickets are inexpensive and you're right on top of the game.

Also, the guidelines for major league hats don't apply to the minor leagues. Hats in the minors go for it. They're usually quirky and charming. This hat has so much weird in it. I'm not sure why they decided to put both eyes and a paw on the logo. I also don't know why the paw is wrecking the ball. That's an illegal pitch. You can get thrown out of the game for that!

All I know is that I love this hat and I wore it a lot. It was a great match with my black and gold softball jersey from the work team.

Milwaukee Brewers
Style: unstructured, strapback
Giveaway at a Brewers game in 2001.

In 2001, Dave and I organized a baseball trip with four friends to go to Milwaukee and Chicago. We wanted to see the Brewers' new stadium.

Miller Park is off the highway, but not close to any bars or restaurants, so it's accessible but isolated. In fact, the only one who has a place to go drinking is the team's mascot, Bernie Brewer, who hangs out in a chalet next to the scoreboard. When the Brewers hit a home run, he slides into a gigantic mug of beer. Talk about being overserved. The Brewers' new home had a retractable roof—like the SkyDome. Unlike the SkyDome, the panels spread open in the middle, rather than sliding over the top. Accommodating this structure makes this stadium feel huge. I think it overwhelms the action.

With the roof closed, the stadium kind of looks like Professor X's power amplification helmet. In the first season in Milwaukee, they'd close the roof at the end of the game. Fans stayed to watch. While we looked at the panels make their slow journey, a guy behind me said, "Wow, this could only happen in America."

I turned around and said, "They've had a retractable roof in Toronto for twelve years."

He thought about it for a second and replied, "It was probably American technology."

Guys like that are the reason my family got such a rocky reception in Canada. I let the comment slide because I knew anything that came out of my mouth next wouldn't be helpful.

This hat was a giveaway that day. It's the lightest hat I own, perfect for running.

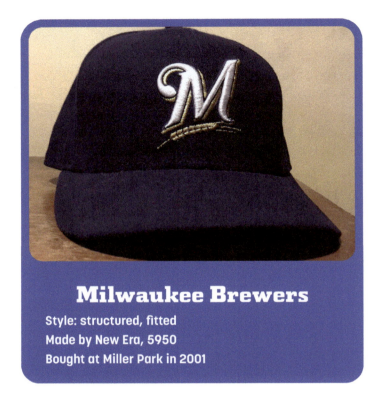

Milwaukee Brewers
Style: structured, fitted
Made by New Era, 5950
Bought at Miller Park in 2001

Yes, I'd already been given a free hat that day but I bought this anyway. I now had several Milwaukee hats despite being indifferent to the Brewers. If you want to take me to task for the number of hats I have, start here. This is a nice hat though. I like the wheat below the M in a muted gold. Also— just three colors. Well done, Brewers. Classy look.

We saw the Brewers play the Braves from seats about five rows above third base. Atlanta won 14-2. Braves starter John Burkett struck out three times on nine pitches. He didn't even move. I've never seen anyone put less effort into anything. If a vulture landed on his bat, I wouldn't have been surprised.

Six guys were supposed to go on the trip, but one dropped out at the last minute. His name was Billy Graham. Really. We decided he needed to be there in some form, so we bought a small stuffed figure to be his proxy.

Between innings, the Brewers have sausage races, where people in bratwurst costumes run around the outfield track.

Stuffed versions of all the racers are sold in the gift shop. We bought the stuffed Hot Dog and called him Little Billy. He came with us everywhere on that trip but wasn't always treated well.

Our next stop was Chicago to see the White Sox play the Rays. After the game, we went back to our hotel, down the street from Buddy Guy's Legends, a great blues bar. Little Billy came along. Dave and I took pictures of him against the Chicago skyline and underneath the wheel of a taxicab as we walked to the entrance, giggling the entire way.

The bouncer, seated outside the door, had been watching us. As we walked into the club, this huge man said in a flat baritone, "You guys sure are having a lot of fun with that doll."

Well, we were.

Cedar Rapids Kernels
Style: structured, fitted
Made by New Era 5950
Bought in Cedar Rapids in 2001

In 2001, I was in Iowa shooting the cereal episode of a food series called "Science to Go" in 2001. After a day of shooting at the Quaker Oats factory in Cedar Rapids, Iowa, the production crew and I headed to a Cedar Rapids Kernels game. The Kernels have played in Iowa since 1890. In 2001, they were the Angels' A league team. The park is small and charming. I was so close to the action I felt like I should be wearing a uniform.

It was an odd game. The Kernels' manager and hitting coach were tossed in the eighth for arguing with the umpire. The paper the next day had the details. The umpire admitted he was making bad calls against the Kernels but told the Kernels' manager it was because one of the team's outfielders had showed him up earlier in the game by demonstrably protesting a call. The ump also said he was furious because he wouldn't be working the playoffs and wouldn't be back the next season. However, a female umpire would be doing both. The rogue umpire wasn't very happy about that either.

Sounds like the league made a good decision. They might have held off on telling him until the season was over though.

I love this hat. It has classic colors and a baseball coming out of a corn stalk.

Fire Department New York
Style: structured, Velcro strapback
Bought in New York City in November 2001

On 9/11, I stood in the "@discovery.ca" newsroom and watched the twin towers of the World Trade Center fall. Everyone working in long-form documentary and factual series dropped what they were doing and volunteered to help put the daily news show together.

I was assigned the lead item—recapping the day's events. I stared at my computer screen, not knowing what to write. That doesn't happen to me often. I asked myself, "What actually happened today?"

The events were so overwhelming, I decided to go through them one at a time. One airplane hitting one tower alone was inconceivable. After a minute, I wrote: "Just after the start of the workday in New York City, one of the worst events in aviation history occurred. Then things got worse."

I then stepped through the series of events. My last line was: "An hour after the first airplane hit, the second tower fell, forever changing the physical, political, and emotional landscape of the United States." That last line turned out to be an understatement. The whole world changed.

In November, Mark Foerster, a hilarious and hard-working cameraman, and I were in New York City for another "Science to Go" shoot. We went to Ground Zero to get a sense of the tragedy. A block away, we saw the jagged edge of one of the broken buildings pointing into the sky. The smell of burnt electrical wire still hung in the air. This was two months after 9/11. The rubble was still burning.

Clean-up had barely begun. I knew that the bodies of office workers, police officers, and firefighters were still buried a short distance away. Death was as present as concrete and cool air. It was haunting. As Mark and I walked back, we came across a man selling these hats. I bought it to remind me of the people who ran into the unstable towers that tragic day. It's a symbol of true heroism. I wear this on the Fourth of July.

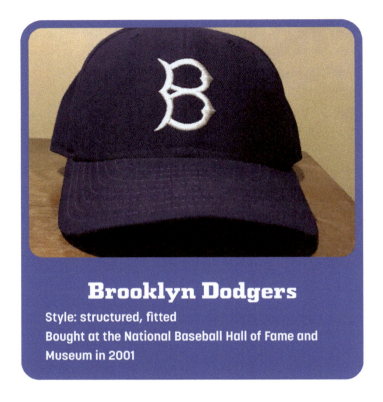

Brooklyn Dodgers
Style: structured, fitted
Bought at the National Baseball Hall of Fame and Museum in 2001

After our shoot in New York City, Mark flew out to another location with a different director. I drove his van back to Toronto, and on the way back, stopped in Cooperstown, New York. It was a chance to visit the National Baseball Hall of Fame and Museum, something I'd always wanted to do.

Cooperstown is a hamlet with a main street that makes you homesick for an idealized past. Main Street is like a living Norman Rockwell painting. Wally and Beaver Cleaver should live around the corner. Little shops with baseball souvenirs line the walk between the tiny ballpark, where I parked, and the Hall of Fame.

The museum itself is stately but understated. Three arches in a brick facade welcome you to the history of America's past time. Displays from the earliest days of the game, ragged balls and puffy gloves, through its greatest moments, are revealed on a casual stroll through several levels. The museum is exactly what you want it to be, a distillation of America's pastime.

For me, the highlight was the Jackie Robinson exhibit, a tribute to the man who broke baseball's color barrier. One of the letters he received is on display. It wasn't from a fan.

This star athlete's spectacular play while facing blistering racism is one of the greatest achievements in sports history. I can't imagine the personal toll it took. Jackie Robinson helped integrate not just baseball, but society itself. His courage lifted us all. We owe him a debt. I bought this cap of the Brooklyn Dodgers, Robinson's team, to remind me of his accomplishments.

Brooklyn was the first team to wear a baseball-style hat instead of a straw hat back in the 1860s, although it looked more like a jockey's cap. By the 1900s, the baseball cap was called the Brooklyn-style cap. The white B is round and friendly, a tip of its hat to the warm relationship the team had with its Brooklyn home. The royal blue is warm and confident.

If you love baseball hats, you probably love this gorgeous icon, too.

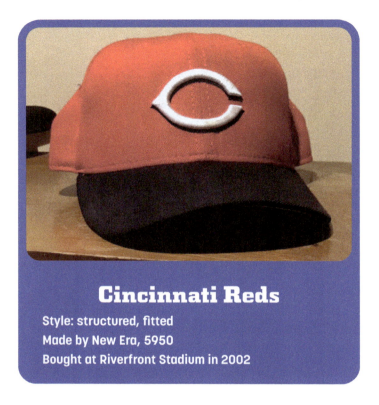

Cincinnati Reds
Style: structured, fitted
Made by New Era, 5950
Bought at Riverfront Stadium in 2002

In April 2002, Larry and I celebrated the start of the baseball season with a quick two-day trip to Cincinnati and Cleveland. Riverfront Stadium was in its final season, and I wanted to see it, even though hosting the Big Red Machine's back-to-back championships in the 1970s was the stadium's only claim to fame.

Some teams get their identity from one glorious moment in their existence. The Reds are like that for me. Even when they field poor teams, I always think of those outstanding Reds World Series legends when I hear the team's name or see their colors. Perhaps that's unfair to a team that started in the 1880s and has won nine National League Pennants and five World Series, but the Big Red Machine was a rare beast. Every position player was an all-star.

Riverfront Stadium was another matter. It was one of those concrete, multipurpose monstrosities that cropped up like a rash of huge, ugly hat boxes in the 1960s. They were all mercifully replaced when the gorgeous, trendsetting, revenue machine, Camden Yards, debuted in Baltimore. Riverfront Stadium was everything I expected—ugly. Still, this was part of baseball history and worth checking out.

The game we saw, against the Colorado Rockies, was delayed for an hour and a half by a spectacular thunderstorm. Larry and I watched the lightning show from our 200-level seats under the overhang. When the shower ended, the stadium was almost empty, so we moved right behind the visitor's batting circle. Larry Walker of the Rockies talked to fans from Colorado who were sitting beside us. Juan Encarnacion drove in the winning run for the Reds in the bottom of the ninth. We were cheering so loud our heads hurt.

The next stop on our trip, Jacob's Field in Cleveland, was gorgeous, built in the same style as Camden Yards. I didn't buy a hat, however, because I found Cleveland's logo offensive. I've met Indigenous people who like it, and I respect their feelings, but after what I'd seen growing up in Thunder Bay, I just couldn't put that caricature on my head.

St. Louis Cardinals
Style: structured, fitted
Made by New Era, 5950
Bought at Busch Stadium in 2002

By 2002, the summer baseball trip with my friends from Thunder Bay had become an annual event. Our next destination was to St. Louis, one of the great baseball cities.

It took two days to get there. We'd stopped taking our work authority with us. Leaving that behind meant the trips were pure joy, a chance to shrug off our adult responsibilities and fill our friendship tank. There's nothing like being in the presence of people who have known you at your most awkward and vulnerable. Barriers drop and you can just be. Some nicknames flew around the van. Paul called me Pushy McMyway. I liked it. It felt like permission.

Dave loved the trip conversations. He'd drop a topic, then sit back, smiling, as everyone got worked up. Once, after someone made a particularly impassioned point, I said "Yeah, you're probably right." Dave looked disappointed. "You can't do that!" he retorted.

As the conversations became more animated, so did Dave, laughing and busting out opinions. He was either the quietest loud guy or the loudest quiet guy I'd ever known, I could never decide which.

One of the great moments of this trip was seeing the St. Louis Arch in the distance. I love the feeling of approaching. It tingles with anticipation. We all leaned forward as the Arch grew bigger in the windshield. After we checked into the hotel, we drank beer in the lobby bar wearing Hawaiian shirts.

Old Busch Stadium was another concrete cookie-cutter, but the Cardinals—the most successful franchise in the National League with nineteen National League pennants and eleven World Series titles—found a way to make one of these eyesores tolerable. Natural grass had replaced AstroTurf and arches decorated the rim of the upper deck. It may not be the prettiest stadium, but it works.

The Cardinals are a self-assured team. They're the well-dressed, highly skilled co-worker everyone goes to when the job needs to be done right. Even their mistakes seem minor because they do so many things well so much of the time. That is especially true of their uniforms.

The Cardinals' jerseys have the most ornate logo in baseball, two cardinals perched on either end of a bat with Cardinals in script hanging below. Even during the powder-blue pajama pullover days in the 1970s, the Cardinals somehow managed to look timeless. Their hats are perfection. The interlocking white STL is smartly proportioned, lined with a thin black border, resting on a bold red field. I couldn't wait to get one.

The sea of red hats and clothing in the stands creates a celebratory atmosphere. Cardinals' fans understand the game, too. They pay attention and know when to cheer. I'm sure Cubs fans think the Cardinals fans are smug, but it's earned.

We sat on the first-base side in the upper deck, watching the famous Arch peering over the top of the stadium. It was crazy hot. I thought I was going to get a heat stroke, and we were at a night game. The Cardinals thumped their archrivals the Cubs that night 8-4.

After the game, we crossed the street and stood outside a bar under the highway, waiting for the shuttle bus. It was a long wait, so I bought some tall boys out of an ice bucket, and we drank them as we watched a girl in a red tank top have an uncomfortable conversation with her less-than-concerned boyfriend. We took turns guessing what the dispute was about. We all agreed, it was his fault.

The next day, after another Cards/Cubs game, we started the journey home. Music was a big part of these trips. We'd pick the song of the trip and the other songs that would appear on the CD I would later make as a souvenir for my friends. The CD cover always had a picture of Little Billy at the Stadium, the name of the trip, and a picture of all of us on the back.

In the middle we'd have the track listing and usually a picture of a server at a restaurant with Little Billy. This trip was called "Missouri Loves Company." There was no waitress inside the place we stopped at for a breakfast buffet, so I included a picture from the sign outside the restaurant. It said, "All You Care to Eat." The sign was accurate. No one cared to eat much of that terrible buffet.

The song of the trip was "Gypsies, Tramps, and Thieves," by Cher. I have no idea why a van full of guys would pick that song except that we all sang it at the top of our lungs. Good tune.

We caught a Jays/Twins game in Minnesota on the way. This was not a trip for beautiful stadiums. More on the Metrodome, the worst stadium ever, later.

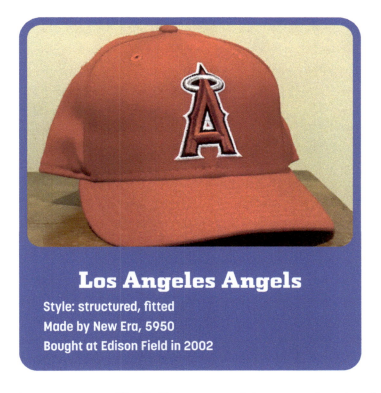

Los Angeles Angels
Style: structured, fitted
Made by New Era, 5950
Bought at Edison Field in 2002

Later that summer, Mark Foerster and I were in Los Angeles on one of the last shoots for Season Three of "The Sex Files." For the episode on future sex, we visited a company that made adult films, but had also developed a sensory suit that could be activated by a partner remotely, for long-distance relationships.

It's not unusual for companies to send production crews home with a gift, so we all walked out with some DVDs. Personally, I find these films boring, but it would have been rude to say no. They found out that I'm a huge Bruce Springsteen fan and invited me to Las Vegas to see the Boss with them in a private box. Sadly, I had to say no to that one. The concert was the night before we flew back, and I would have had to drive straight back to LA after the show. A sleepless night at the wheel felt even more dangerous than hanging out with the porn producers.

We also did a shoot with a bedroom toy producer. They also offered us a gift, and, again, I didn't want to be rude. It was the last thing I threw in my suitcase before the flight back.

I've been pulled over at customs exactly once. This was the time. I was waved into the baggage search room with my little gifts from LA—porn and a sex toy—right on top of my clothing.

Remember what I said about how much I love anticipation? Not this time. I was running through explanations in my head when a female officer in her late twenties came by. She looked at my declaration card.

"Do you know why you've been pulled over?"

"Nope."

"You spent more than your limit. You weren't out of the country for a week."

"Oh, I'm sorry. Does that mean you have to search my bag?"

She looked me in the eyes. I did my best to seem nonchalant.

"No, just don't let it happen again."

I grabbed my suitcase full of depravity and got the hell out of there.

The trip wasn't all devilry though. Mark and I saw the Angels play Cleveland at Edison Field. The Angels are the friendly B student who joins a few extracurriculars. They do a lot of things right, but not enough to get a scholarship. Their uniforms have always been nice. They even stitched a halo on their cap at one point, a clever trick.

They've had great players—Nolan Ryan, Rod Carew, Reggie Jackson, Mike Trout, Shohei Otani—and a clever logo, with a halo on the A, but they had yet to win a pennant or World Series when I saw them. Both would come later that year. The Angels are likeable, you just wish they could do better.

Mark and I sat in the last row of the lower deck in rightfield. The stadium is nice but unremarkable. The boulder garden in centerfield is a good touch. After the game, we watched one of the best fireworks displays I'd ever seen. Thanks Disney. The Happiest Place on Earth was right next door.

This hat is the only souvenir I kept from the trip.

Shakespeare's Globe
Style: structured, Velcro strapback

The summer of 2002 wasn't entirely spent in ballparks. Nancy and I were in London, England, for two days before a two-week holiday in Ireland with our friend Laura. We spent one of those days at Shakespeare's Globe, a faithful recreation of the theatre where the Bard originally staged his plays.

I love Shakespeare. His wordplay is astounding—complex sentence structures support stunning metaphors and observations:

> "But wait, what's that light in the window over there?
> It is the east, and Juliet is the sun.
> Rise up, beautiful sun, and kill the jealous moon."
> —Romeo and Juliet

> "I could be well moved if I were as you.
> If I could pray to move, prayers would move me.
> But I am constant as the northern star,

Of whose true-fixed and resting quality
There is no fellow in the firmament." —Julius Caesar

"Tomorrow, and tomorrow, and tomorrow,
Creeps in this petty pace from day to day
To the last syllable of recorded time,
And all our yesterdays have lighted fools
The way to dusty death." —Macbeth

The incredible phrasing informs stories filled with conflicted characters revealing the breadth of human experience. Sometimes I travel with his complete works, just to flip through a few scenes in down time. I much prefer the tragedies and histories, but "A Midsummer Night's Dream" was the only play we had a chance to see at the Globe. Fortunately, it's my favorite of his comedies. Despite being more than 400 years old, it's still laugh-out-loud funny.

The theatre is like a small stadium, white on the outside with wooden seats on the inside in a circle around the stage. The performance area itself is minimalist, as it would have been during Shakespeare's day. There is a pit in front of the stage on a dirt floor for the commoners. We had bench seats in the second level. I would have been happy anywhere. It was like sitting in a time machine. At least it was until the performers took the stage in pajamas. The production was playful and hilarious. It was a thrill to walk around the gorgeous building, absorbing the context in which Shakespeare's creations were originally presented.

I love the hat, although I didn't buy it at the theatre. It was given to me years later by my Discovery Channel colleague and Down Home Blues teammate, David Smillie, who shared my love of the Bard.

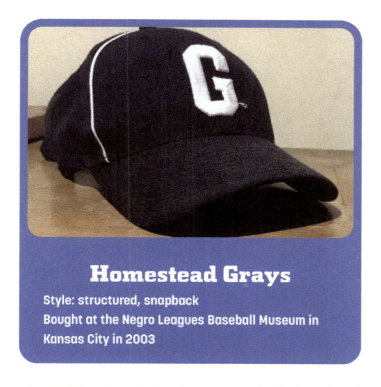

Homestead Grays
Style: structured, snapback
Bought at the Negro Leagues Baseball Museum in Kansas City in 2003

Our most ambitious baseball trip was in 2003. We drove from Thunder Bay to Kansas City, Missouri, seeing five games in three days. The usual trip mates, Dave, John Petrynka, Phil Whalley, Paul Manary, Little Billy, and I were joined by my close friend John O'Gorman, who flew in from B.C. to join us on the drive. I was especially excited about JohnO's inclusion. He's one of my best friends and has my favorite characteristics—smart, funny, and opinionated.

JohnO established his presence immediately. As we pulled out of Thunder Bay, before the sun was up, I put on a mixed CD I'd made just for the occasion. It started with a mellow song, to match the morning mood. About ten seconds in, JohnO exclaimed, "What kind of a road-trip song is this?"

Who invited this guy? Stupid rookie.

I'd added a Bob Marley song to the CD, just for JohnO. When "I Shot the Sheriff" came on, JohnO said, "This is my least favorite Bob Marley song. I've never liked it." Kansas City started to look even farther away.

As an added bonus for my tripmates, I got a cold and lost my voice the night before we left. As we pulled out of Thunder Bay, the guys were already calling it the best trip ever.

They were right. On the first day, we saw Cleveland play Minnesota in Minneapolis in the afternoon. That night, in Des Moines, we saw the Salt Lake Stingers play the Iowa Cubs, Chicago's AAA team.

That night at the hotel, the room was filled with the synergy of drinks and opinions. To establish order, Dave made a hat out of a paper bag and wore it as a sign that he had the floor. Then he would point to someone, granting them a turn to talk. The evening was only enhanced by Dave's shabby imperialism.

The next day, we saw the Twins play the Royals in Kansas City. On our last day, we watched the second game of that series in the afternoon and then saw the Vikings play the Chiefs in a preseason game that night. In between, we went to B.B.'s Barbecue, a blues club with a barbecue pit from the 1950s. They served the best ribs I'd ever eaten.

John Petrynka accidentally dressed like an umpire. He had a black hat and black shorts with a powder blue button up shirt. We eventually told him what he looked like, but only after a couple of hours of asking questions like, "Hey JP, is it SAFE to park here?" "Is this the way OUT?" You're only young once, but you can be immature forever.

When we woke up, Dave said to me, "Hey, you need to have a sleep test."

"Why?"

"Because you stop breathing at night. You snore, stop, fight for air, then start breathing again. It happens all night."

Dave was describing sleep apnea. He knew what he was talking about because he had it, too. Every night, he strapped a mask on his face that forced air through his nose down his throat to keep his windpipe open. Even with that help, Dave didn't sleep well and was awake a lot at night. I had it checked out later and he was right. Dave's advice extended my life.

The highlight of the trip for me was the Negro League Baseball Museum. Too many great players haven't received their due because shortsighted people couldn't see past the pigmentation of a millimeter of skin. It's shameful and infuriating. At this museum, Negro League Players shine. I bought this Homestead Grays hat in honor of Josh Gibson, my pick for best player of all time. His power numbers rival Babe Ruth and his batting average is about the same as Ty Cobb. And he did it playing catcher.

If you're a sports fan and land in Kansas City, you must go.

Kansas City Royals
Style: structured, fitted
Made by New Era, 5950
Bought in Toronto in 2003

The Kansas City Royals are like the Los Angeles Dodgers' little brother. I'd read that the Royals organization was modeled on the Dodgers but haven't been able to confirm that. It makes sense, though. Both teams have the same color scheme, and their nickname is written in script across their chest. Both are smart and classy. The Royals just don't have any money, so their droughts between winning seasons are much longer.

Also, both of their stadiums still hold up today. When the lovely Kauffman Stadium opened in 1973, it was an anomaly. While other baseball teams partnered with football teams to build concrete, multipurpose hat boxes, the Royals opted for a purpose-built baseball stadium.

There are fountains in the outfield and a scoreboard with a huge crown. The Royals should be commended for their foresight. Now before we get too gushy, they did have AstroTurf for twenty years, but by the time we arrived, that abomination was long gone.

We saw two games, a night game and a day game. The day game was scorching. We had great seats five rows deep in the upper deck behind home plate, but we moved way back into the shade. Sweat was pouring over my sunglasses. The team made the vendors wear long black pants, even under a blistering sun. A beer vendor passed out and was removed by paramedics.

Dave caught a hot dog shot out of a cannon by the Royals' mascot, a muscular lion. The bun liquified in the heat. I can't believe he ate it.

The Royals' backup catcher, Mike DiFelice, who played about once a week, freaked out over a disputed call in the first inning. He threw a Gatorade jug and a bunch of equipment onto the field. DiFelice was tossed out of the game. I was sure he did it on purpose to get out of the heat. There's no way the everyday catcher was happy about that.

I looked around the gift shops for a Royals 5950 cap, but there was none to be found. What the hell, Royals?

I looked at some other options, consulting with Dave on how they looked. He frowned and shook his head. "If you're going to spend the money for a hat, you should get the one you want."

Dave was right. I passed on the available options and found this one at a sports store in Toronto. I'm glad I waited. The 5950 hat is the top of the line, and I'm glad I didn't settle, especially on a hat as nice as the Royals'. The royal blue with a stylishly integrated KC is so classy it would look at home on a wedding invitation. The white button on top is a nice touch, too.

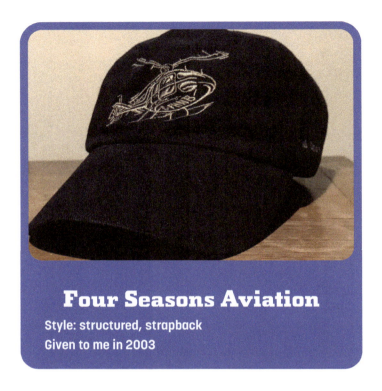

Four Seasons Aviation
Style: structured, strapback
Given to me in 2003

Helicopter shoots are routine for some of my colleagues. I had just one helicopter flight, in 2003, over Niagara Falls. It was for a series I was producing called "Ultimate Access," which took viewers behind the scenes of high-profile places. For one glorious afternoon, I got to ride in a helicopter over the iconic landmark.

It was a gorgeous, sunny day. The chopper ascended over the Rainbow Bridge, just shy of the American and Canadian Falls, then flew over the rim of cascading water, again and again. Since I was directing, I had to keep my eye on the monitor as we flew over the edge of the falls. Our shots were spectacular.

We arrived back in Toronto at night, and since we'd paid for the day, we flew around the CN Tower and took shots of the Air Canada Centre, the site of our episode about the behind-the-scenes action at a Toronto Raptors game.

Dave Tommasini, the owner and pilot, either got a sense of how buzzed I was, or I thanked him a little too effusively. For whatever reason, he gave me one of his hats. I love it. It's so TV industry.

The day was a thrill. I was literally flying high. My job allowed me to do exciting things, be creative, and lead a talented team. I was married to a smart, beautiful, fun woman. Everything was going my way in life. Of course, I felt like I deserved it and that it would last forever. Neither was true.

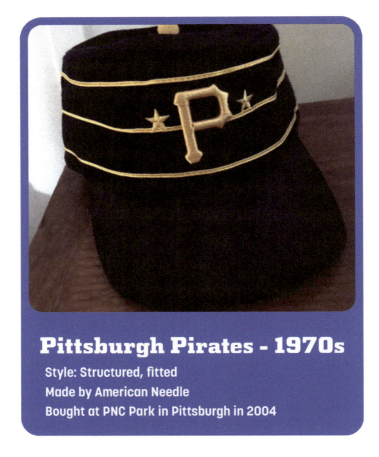

Pittsburgh Pirates - 1970s
Style: Structured, fitted
Made by American Needle
Bought at PNC Park in Pittsburgh in 2004

Dave and I picked Cleveland, Cincinnati, and Pittsburgh as destinations for our 2004 baseball trip. This adventure was unusual for a few reasons.

We left from Toronto, not Thunder Bay. Some new participants came along, as well. Dave, Paul Manary, and I were joined by our high school friend Tim Cattani, my Discovery Channel colleague Larry, and my pal Marc Stevens.

Most importantly, we went in May instead of later in the summer because Nancy and I were expecting our first child in June.

Of the trip rookies, Tim stood out. He ignited a few farts for our entertainment and his foot was run over by a cab. Larry did his best to keep up by closing the car door on Dave's finger. Marc just drank a lot of Diet Coke.

In Cleveland, we went to the Rock & Roll Hall of Fame, where I saw Bruce Springsteen's handwritten lyrics to "Jungleland." The T-shirt, jeans, black studded belt, and red cap the Boss wore on the cover of "Born in the USA" were on display along with outfits from Mick Jagger, Elton John, and Earth, Wind and Fire. Dave wasn't impressed. He called the museum "old laundry."

Then we went for dinner where Dave insisted that I order an Arrogant Bastard Ale. I did and liked it. You might not, though. It's not for everyone.

At night we saw Cleveland play Boston with CC Sabathia pitching for Cleveland against Pedro Martinez for the Red Sox. Our seats were behind home plate, midway up the lower deck. Pedro and the Red Sox won 4-3.

The next night we had seats behind home plate about a third of the way up in the upper deck at Great American Ball Park—the new stadium in Cincinnati. It's another brick-and-steel-beauty filled with festive, all-red seats. We could see a riverboat cruising down the Ohio River beyond centerfield.

Ken Griffey Jr. and the Reds hosted Barry Bonds and the Giants. A grade-school class was sitting behind us for this great matchup. The game was scoreless through six innings. In the top of the seventh with two outs, the Reds walked Barry Bonds. The next batter, Pedro Feliz, hit a two-run homer.

After that, the school kids started filing past us.

"Hey, where are you going?" I asked a few students walking by. "There's plenty of game left."

A little girl about twelve years-old yelled back, bent over in anger, "We don't want to go. The teachers are making us!"

I said to Dave, "Well, that's not right."

As the teachers came by, I said, in a friendly tone, "Heading out already?"

One teacher replied casually, "Yeah, it's a school night so we're getting them on the bus."

I leaned forward and belted out: "BOOOOOOOOOOO!"

People joined me. The teachers hung their heads as they ducked out. They had it coming. You can't take kids to a game like that and make them leave early. The Giants won 6-1.

The next night we saw the Dodgers beat the Pirates 4-3 in Pittsburgh. We had seats behind home plate near the back of the lower deck.

At the gift shop, I looked over this throwback stovepipe Pirates hat, but was hesitant about buying it, so I asked Dave what he thought.

"What will you be doing when you wear it?" he asked.

"Playing softball," I replied. The company softball team's colors were black and gold.

"Get it," Dave said. It was the right call. I love this cap's old-time feel.

We drove back to Toronto the next morning in time to see a Blue Jays afternoon game. We watched the Jays beat the White Sox 5-2 from the upper deck behind home plate. This game was a bonus, an afterthought to another carefully planned trip by Dave and me. I didn't realize how significant it would be.

My first son Shane was born a little more than a month later. Baseball trips would never be the same after that.

Detroit Tigers—Home
Style: structured, fitted
Made by New Era, 5950

At 4:30 a.m. on June 13, 2004, my wife woke me up. Her water had broken. I put on this hat, we picked up our bags, already packed, a boom box, and some CDs, and headed for the hospital, after a quick stop at Larry's house to drop off the bases and bats for that night's baseball game. Nancy likes to tease me about that detour, but the team couldn't play the game without the gear. It's not like she was ready to deliver in the car.

When we arrived at the maternity ward, no one was at reception. That wasn't comforting. The last thing you want to see when you're about to have a baby is an unattended hospital. After a quick search, someone let us in.

My mom told us walking would make the baby come faster, so we started marching around the hallway while I timed and recorded the contractions in a notebook. I liked that. I was used to documenting things. One particularly big contraction sent us back to the delivery room where we requested, and received, an epidural.

The next hours were a blur. I did my best to be helpful in the delivery room, icing down Nancy's neck and saying what I hoped were encouraging words, but I felt useless. Watching the love of your life suffer is gut wrenching, the worst thing I had ever seen. Fortunately, the worst thing I had ever seen was followed by the best. At 12:47 p.m., our child emerged, bright red and crying. I yelled, "It's a boy!" The nurses took him over to the scale to weigh him. I looked at Nancy. She said, "Go with him!" How could she be more composed than I was?

I took a few pictures of our newest family member. I swore I wouldn't gush. I knew the child that came out of my wife would be squashed and kind of weird looking. But when I saw my son, stretching out as far as he could on the scale, I thought, "I've never seen anything so beautiful." The nurses swaddled the baby and put him in my arms. I indulged myself for just a few seconds. Nancy deserved the cuddle time.

I handed our child to my shockingly relaxed wife. I was in awe of her. Nancy looked up at me, and calmly said, "So, Shane?"

We had agreed on only two boys' names. I was so rattled, I thought she was stating a preference, not asking a question. I said, "OK."

Then Nancy asked, "What about a middle name?"

I replied with the only answer that made sense to me after watching my wife push another human out of her body: "Whatever you want."

Nancy chose Adderley, her family name, in honor of her late father.

For the rest of the day and all through the night we looked at Shane and listened to him murmur. "Meh, muh, mi." He was already trying to talk. That would never stop.

There aren't many times your life changes in a moment. My life has two volumes, one before this and one after. The sequel is by far the superior story. I love being a dad. And I didn't know it then, but that boy was about to save me.

Thunder Bay Border Cats
Style: structured, fitted
Made by Zephyr
Bought in 2005.

In 2004 a new baseball team arrived in Thunder Bay. This one was in the Northwoods League, a summer league for college players. Before the games, little leaguers joined the team on the field for the introductions. Dave immediately signed up his boys, Ryan, nine, and Ben, seven. He did everything for his boys. In turn, they idolized him. To Ryan and Ben, Dave was as essential as oxygen.

I didn't go to a Border Cats game in 2004. That waited until the following year.

In June 2005, I quit Discovery Channel. It was time to spread my wings as a freelance producer. Without realizing what the other was doing, two executives at the same production company, Cineflix, each offered me a job producing a series. The owner of the company intervened to determine who would get me. Between my last week at Discovery and my first at Cineflix, I would go on the annual baseball trip with Dave and our friends. The planned stops were Philadelphia, Washington, and Baltimore. I was riding high.

It didn't last.

On June twenty-third, a week before I was to leave Discovery, I called Dave in the morning to talk about the trip. I couldn't reach him.

At 5:15 p.m., I got a call at work from Thunder Bay. It was Dave's cousin, Lisa Brygidyr.

"Dave's gone," she whispered.

"What? What does that mean?"

"Dave's dead."

"What? How? What happened?"

Lisa didn't want to tell me, but I pressed.

"I'm not some guy, Lisa. I'm part of the family."

Lisa relented. Dave had lost a battle to depression.

The drive home took every ounce of concentration I had.

"Just get home," I repeated in my head.

I walked in the door and up the stairs. Nancy was in our bedroom with Shane. She knew something was wrong the second she saw me.

"Dave's dead," I said, then sank to the floor and sobbed. Nancy rushed Shane to his crib then tried to console me.

I didn't compose myself in time to catch the last flight to Thunder Bay that night, but I booked one for the next morning. I saw Relita's brother and his family at the airport. Everyone was in a gray haze.

From the departure gate, I called my boss at work. I told him where I was going and why and that I didn't know when I'd be back. To his credit, he told me to do what I had to do.

I made myself one promise. I wasn't going home to be a tourist. I was going to help the family, to do what Dave would expect of me. What I would expect of him. Fortunately, the Hagbergs wanted me to be part of the process.

The following week was a blur of tragic activities. Dave's sister, Val, was shredded. Dave's father, Darcy, told me how he had found Dave's body. Darcy and I went to the police station to retrieve Dave's final note. I helped the family write the obituary and read it to his children while Ryan sat on my knee. The family asked me to write the eulogy.

At the end of each day, I'd get in my parents' car. Since I was finally alone, I'd cry. Then I'd drive to my parents' house, talk to my mom and dad, and take calls from my family. Everyone was devastated. Dave was part of our family, too. My family was worried about me and became more worried when they didn't hear from me during the day. Nancy said it was like I was diving into deep water, and no one knew what was happening to me down there.

After taking calls from Nancy and my brothers, I'd work on the eulogy. I knew these would be the most important words I'd ever say and that I wouldn't have time to craft them.

Being in Dave's world without Dave was surreal, but some normal activities continued. Ryan was pitching in a baseball game that week. Dave's oldest son was crazy about the sport and wasn't going to miss his chance to start. He told me I had to be there.

"Don't let me down. I'm counting on you."

The whole family watched that brave ten-year-old out on the mound. Everyone at the park knew he was battling more than opposing batters. Ryan pitched well.

I also took the boys to a Border Cats game, where I bought this hat. Any distraction was welcome. We watched in the warm summer air, but I couldn't concentrate on the action.

The next day we held the viewing of Dave's body, the low point in a week of crushing grief. Dave wore my dad's black mock turtleneck underneath a Bruins jersey I had given him. My best friend's face looked pale and pained. As some of Dave's favorite songs played in the background, his friends and family moved through a thick fog of suffering. There was no comfort to be found in this room.

At the end of the viewing, Ryan didn't want to leave Dave's side. For me, this was the worst in a week of devastating moments. The only task I wasn't up to was taking Ryan away from his final moments with his father.

The minister finally stepped up and told Ryan it was time to go. As Ryan turned away from the casket, I told him, "Everything you love about your father is already with you."

When everyone cleared the room, I walked up to Dave's body, and put my hand on his chest.

I said, "It's going to be all right, Dave. We're going to look after everything."

Then I walked away, hoping I could live up to that promise.

The church was packed for the funeral. Speakers were set up outside and in the basement to accommodate the huge crowd of mourners. I rehearsed the eulogy as many times as I could to prevent myself from losing it.

Near the end of the service, I stood in front of Dave's loved ones to try to make sense of his life and the tragedy we were living. For twenty minutes, I told stories I'd gathered from Dave's friends and family. I tried to have a moment for each of the people closest to him.

I talked about how our friendship had shaped my life, how we had made each other better people. No amount of loss could diminish the gifts Dave's life had given me. Then I told everyone about Dave's wordless hug the night before I left for university, when our lives were changing, and we were forced to say goodbye.

After I finished, I sat next to my parents in the pew and exhaled. Relita looked over to me and said, "I love you."

Dave wasn't put in the ground that day. Only a handful of us were there for that moment, a few days later. Darcy wanted to put his son's ashes in the grave. There was no ceremony, just the quiet tragedy of watching a man put the remains of his child into a hole in the dirt.

Dave was forty-two years old.

We became best friends twenty-seven years earlier, when we were just fifteen. I was skinny with big glasses, but outgoing and fun. Dave was a cool guy in a jean jacket who wore sunglasses in class (they were prescription shades), but he was reserved. We ran for student council together in Grade Ten as a joke, going on stage for our campaign speech in our underwear. We played sports together, were in a band together, were best men at each other's weddings.

A frequent and favorite conversation was how our friendship had brought out parts of each other that might have remained dormant. I helped him open up and he made me less geeky. Dave and I changed each other for the better. When people say you're lucky if you have one friend in life, this is what they mean. I was closer to Dave Hagberg than I was to my brothers.

We talked all the time. Dave was the best listener. When something was bothering me, he'd keep the focus on my issues, asking questions to bring out the thoughts I might bury. Then he'd tell me what I needed to hear, not what I wanted to hear. When something was bothering Dave, he'd talk about it, but only if I asked him directly.

In 1995, before the birth of his first son, Ryan, Dave was really sick. No one knew what was wrong with him. I didn't even know he was ill until my mom and dad said they'd seen Dave and he was thin, 168 pounds. Dave never clocked in under 220.

He hadn't said a word about this to me. When I called Dave and asked what was going on, he opened up. I could tell he was relieved to be able to discuss it with me. Dave was scared. So was I. Eventually, doctors found out he had Crohn's disease, which inflames the digestive tract. Some of his intestines were removed, and Dave controlled the rest with diet. Crisis averted.

I'd always thought that no matter what happened in life, Dave and I would be there for each other. But because of his sleep apnea, he never slept well. Because of his Chrohn's disease, his diet was off. And Dave just wasn't able to ask for help. I don't know what got him in the end, I just knew he was gone.

I would never get over this loss.

Part of me died with Dave.

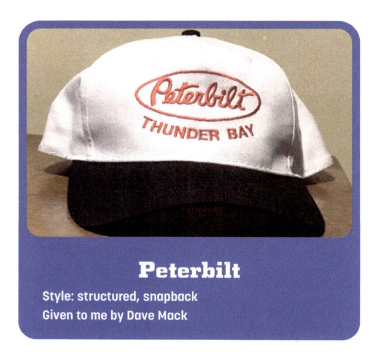

Peterbilt

Style: structured, snapback
Given to me by Dave Mack

Dave Hagberg was Dave Mack's best friend, too. The three of us played football together in high school. Back then, Dave and Dave dated two of the gorgeous Harney sisters. The Daves were both good looking and athletic.

People sometimes told Dave Mack he looked like Patrick Swayze. After high school, Dave Mack (we always called him by both names) went to work for his dad at the Thunder Bay Truck Centre, later becoming part owner. He was the first of us to get married and the first to have kids, three daughters. After the funeral, before I went back to Toronto, Dave Mack and I had a chance to talk alone outside the Hagbergs' house.

Dave Mack told me, "Craig, you had to do what you did here. You couldn't have done anything else."

"I did what Dave would have expected me to do. And I had the easy part. I'm going home. Someone has to look after Dave's family now and that someone is you."

Dave Mack nodded. I wasn't telling him anything he didn't already know.

To no one's surprise, Dave Mack stopped by Dave's house all the time. He coached Ryan and Ben in baseball and hockey. He eventually hired Ben at the truck center.

Dave Mack told me he was able to do so much because his three daughters were older and more independent. I'm sure that's true. I'm also sure Dave Mack would have stepped up anyway.

Years later, Ryan said to me, "I have to hand it to Dave Mack. He really came through for us."

When I flew home after the funeral, I had no idea who would come through for me. I was an inconsolable mess, standing on the edge of a huge crater in my life. I didn't know how big it was or how much damage was done.

I walked in my front door and put down my bag. Shane, just a year old, was playing with a toy underneath the kitchen window, straight ahead, across the length of the house. Shane saw me, dropped the toy, and crawled toward me as fast as he could. Then he pulled himself up on my pantleg, looked up, and stretched out his arms.

I picked him up and held him close.

Shane was always daddy's boy. In the months and years that followed, his need for my attention kept me from sinking into a deep black hole. My little boy saved me.

Dave Mack gave me this hat; I can't remember when. Like Dave Mack, it's solid, dependable, structured, and can adjust when needed.

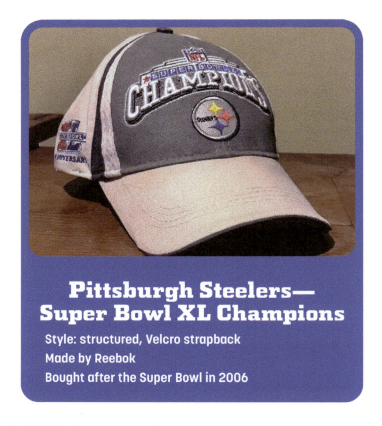

Pittsburgh Steelers— Super Bowl XL Champions

Style: structured, Velcro strapback
Made by Reebok
Bought after the Super Bowl in 2006

In July 2005, I started my first freelance producing job on a new series called "Birth Days." It was about the days immediately before and after a couple has a baby.

I was excited about the topic and the opportunity, but my mind was in a fog. Dave's death hung over everything I did. Producing the first season of a series is the toughest. Despite the most rigorous planning, the first episodes need to be examined thoroughly.

To complicate things, my bosses were in England and wanted to watch every cut of every episode on videotape rather than on a link on their computers. This meant notes on a show could take more than a week to arrive instead of a few hours. The delays in the review process put the series dangerously behind schedule. The long stretches of uncertainty made me question my skills as a producer. We weren't getting the show right and I felt like it was my fault.

The first episode was due on the air in February, and in November, the broadcaster still wasn't happy with the product. Enacting their notes took forever because of our glacial approval process. The air date was approaching without a single show being blessed by the broadcaster. Stress was through the roof.

On top of that, Shane had started daycare and was getting colds with painful ear infections. He'd wake up in the middle of the night crying in pain. Nancy and I would take him to the doctor, they'd prescribe antibiotics, and Shane would sleep. When the antibiotics had run their course, the pain would return. This cycle went on for months.

Work was hell. I was losing confidence in my abilities. Home life was painful. I was wracked with grief. This was the lowest point in my life. One night, I came home, sat down on the kitchen floor, and cried. I thought about leaving television. I was broken.

Fortunately, one wonderful thing happened. The Steelers beat the Seahawks in Super Bowl XL. It was an oasis of relief in a desert of misery. As soon as the championship hats went online, I ordered one.

By this time, "Birth Days" had a new executive producer for about two months. He stayed in Canada for a few weeks, approving cuts and liaising with the broadcaster. When he went back to England, he watched cuts of the show on his computer. This put us back on schedule. The series was finally humming along.

Days after the Super Bowl, I had a job interview with my favorite bosses from Discovery Channel and TSN. They were launching the first high-definition channels in Canada and needed a director of production. I got the job. Soon after, Shane had surgery to put tubes in his ears, which stopped the earaches.

It felt like I was starting to emerge from the darkness, and I had a great-looking new Steelers Super Bowl XL Championship hat. It would be my go-to cap for a long time.

Collector Showdown
Style: unstructured, strapback

I started my new job at High Fidelity HDTV in February 2006. The startup was owned by John Panikkar, Ken Murphy, and David Patterson. We were launching the first four high-definition channels in Canada, although Discovery Channel got their HD offering on air just before we did.

My job was to create programs, hire production teams, oversee production, and review some commissions. We had a co-production deal with a company called Voom, which had just launched twenty HD channels in the United States. Voom executives had to approve all productions before we could start.

In April, our first series, "Collector Showdown," was greenlit. Two collectors would compete in a contest of knowledge and skill for a fabulous mystery prize. I liked the concept, but there were a few caveats. The series needed to be produced in HD, still expensive at the time, for $15k an hour, a pittance, and we needed to have twenty-six episodes fully delivered by the end of December, a tight schedule with a barebones crew, none of whom had been hired. We had a big mountain to climb.

When we shot our first episode, the production team consisted of the producer, Barb Margetts, an excellent lifestyle programming director, and the host, Sonya Buyting, an enthusiastic producer getting her first shot fronting a series. The premiere episode featured two comic book collectors. We shot it at a small comic book convention and the winner was surprised with a $1,000 shopping spree, but they had just ten minutes to spend the money. The loser got a hand-drawn picture of Superman by comics legend George Perez. I loved that episode. It was quirky, fun, and showed the passion of the collectors.

Now we had to produce twenty-five more, for little money almost exclusively in the Toronto area. We added six people and started cranking.

Despite the challenges, we had some inspired episodes. A guitar collector played with Randy Bachman, a race car fanatic rode on an Indy track with Paul Tracy, and a golf collector caddied for a pro golfer on a practice round. We shot an episode with the Pittsburgh Pirates in which the winner and his son played catch with All Star outfielder Jason Bay.

Since participants were collectors, each one got an exclusive "Collector Showdown" hat. Sonya later told me she received fan mail from a mother whose two children watched the show every day when it was repeated. I sent them my last two "Collector Showdown" hats, other than this one.

Despite its limitations, the show is special to me. It's the first series I'd dreamed up that went to air. Our team was filled with hardworking, talented, nice people. Most importantly, this show was the start of the most enjoyable part of an enjoyable career, six glorious years in a leadership role with great bosses and coworkers, in a positive, productive work environment.

Much better shows followed. Some won awards and sold well internationally. When our partner Voom folded, and half our production money vanished with it, we still found ways to make good programs. It all started with "Collector Showdown."

I don't wear this hat often, but I love it.

Detroit Tigers—Home 2006 World Series

Style: structured, fitted
Made by New Era, 5950
Bought at Comerica Park at the 2006 World Series

The Detroit Tigers' return to contention in 2006 provided another much-needed jolt of happiness.

After I left Windsor, the Tigers took a dive in the standings. The stars of the 1984 championship team either left or faded and retired. I still loved my Tigers and took a trip to Detroit almost every year to see them. Still, it's a little sad when your team loses all the time. In 2003, the Tigers lost 119 games, worst in American League history. Yes, I went to see them.

Just three years from that nadir, the Tigers were on a tear that took them all the way to the World Series. Life is better when the Tigers are good. A colleague at High Fidelity HDTV, Crista Bazos, had worked at the Toronto Argonauts and was plugged into the Toronto sports scene. She arranged for me to get World Series tickets through a friend at the Blue Jays.

Scott and I drove to Detroit for Game One and planned to return for Games Six and Seven if necessary. Comerica Park was decked out in World Series logos. It was thrilling. We sat out in leftfield and were by far the loudest people in the section.

Unfortunately, Scott Rolen and Albert Pujols homered to lead the Cardinals to a 7-2 victory over Detroit. That was OK. Scott and I were confident the Tigers would win the Series. If we were really unlucky, we'd be back in Motor City for Game Six and maybe Seven. Our luck was worse than that, though. The Tigers lost in five games, thanks to poor hitting and worse fielding. It was disappointing, but not crushing. That season provided me with a lot of happiness when I needed it most.

I bought two hats, a Tigers 5950 cap with a World Series logo and an unstructured 2006 World Series A. L. Champions hat. Despite losing the series, these are still cool hats to own.

Detroit Tigers 2006 World Series

Style: unstructured, strapback
Made by Twins Enterprises, later to be renamed '47 Brand
Bought at Comerica Park at the 2006 World Series

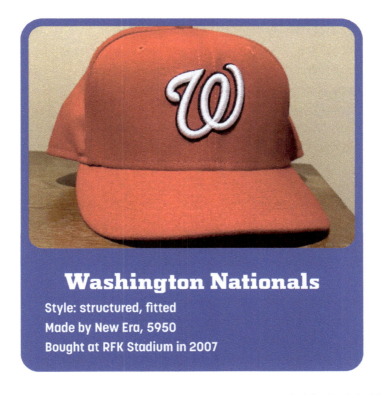

Washington Nationals
Style: structured, fitted
Made by New Era, 5950
Bought at RFK Stadium in 2007

I didn't want the baseball trips to die with Dave. I didn't think he'd want that either. This trip was an important connection to my oldest friends. Without it, I hardly saw them.

So, in 2007, I organized the trip we were supposed to take in 2005. None of my Thunder Bay friends were interested. However, Marc and Larry, who had been on the 2004 trip, signed up. So did my brother Scott and JohnO, who flew in from Vancouver. I think Scott and JohnO came for me. They knew this was a small pilgrimage. Larry brought along a colleague, Chris Blow. He was a writer for some of the shows Larry produced and a big baseball fan. Little Billy came, too.

Our first stop was Baltimore, where the Orioles spanked the Devil Rays 11-6. I did my best to bring Dave along taking small pictures of him with me and leaving them behind at stadiums we visited on the trip. The photos showed him wearing the softball uniform of the team we created, sitting alone against a fence, hat down over his eyes. He's present, but distant, a little obscured. I left one in some potted plants overlooking the outfield. An appropriate spot. His summer job was landscaping.

RFK stadium in Washington was our next stop. What a dump. They poured the concrete and walked away. It felt cold and hollow, even sitting behind home plate near the back of the lower deck. I can't imagine this place was much good for football, either.

At least the Nationals did a good job on the hats. The script W is almost identical to that of the Washington Senators, DC's former team. The black outline makes the white letter stand out on the field of red. As for a team personality, I don't think the Nationals have one yet.

Even without a persona, they played well that day. The Nationals won 6-0. The highlights were Marlins' third baseman Miguel Cabrera making a diving stop. He'd soon become a star for the Tigers. There was also a young woman in front of us who must have watched the game through her right ear. She never looked at the field of play, instead talking to, but not listening to, her neighbor on her left. She didn't even watch the presidents' race. Mascots who look like four former presidents—Abraham Lincoln, Teddy Roosevelt, Thomas Jefferson, and George Washington—race around the edge of the field. Super fun. I tucked a picture of Dave under my seat.

We visited the National Mall and the Vietnam Veterans Memorial, which is stunning. I always cry there. We also stayed at the Watergate Hotel. When we had drinks, I'd pour one for Dave and put it in front of a picture of him.

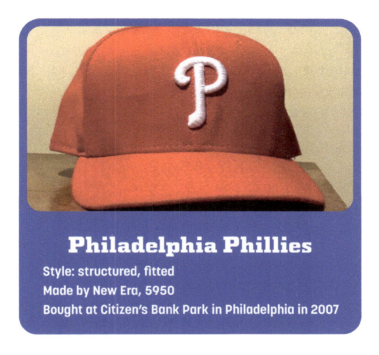

Philadelphia Phillies
Style: structured, fitted
Made by New Era, 5950
Bought at Citizen's Bank Park in Philadelphia in 2007

Our last stop on the baseball trip was Philadelphia, to see the Phillies and Cubs play in Citizen's Bank Park. In the afternoon we visited the Liberty Bell and Independence Hall, where the Declaration of Independence was signed.

Both the bell and document inspire me. Despite the flaws in US history, Americans seeking change could point to both symbols and say, "We're not living up to this promise." It has worked. It needs to keep working.

Most often, teams get their personality from the uniforms, stadium, style of play (when the organization follows a certain philosophy), and their most successful years. The Phillies get their personality from their fan base.

Philadelphia fans' passion often crosses into obnoxious. Soft players don't survive there. Consequently, Philadelphia teams are tough. To me, the Phillies teams throw hard, hit hard, and take no prisoners. I like the hats, but it isn't an ideal match for the Phillies. The P is playful, and the red is bright and positive.

I prefer the Phillies' maroon uniforms from the 1970s, with the curved P incorporating a subtle baseball in the loop. The darker tone made the Phillies look tougher, and with Mike Schmidt, Pete Rose, and Joe Morgan, they were. Maroon is also unique in baseball. I wish they'd switch back. It's a better fit for the city and the team.

The stadium, like all the new stadiums, is brick and steel with wide concourses. It's beautiful. We had seats in the upper deck behind home plate. Unlike other cities, you don't get a nice skyline view because all the Philadelphia teams' playing fields are in one big parking lot outside the city.

It's handy but less fun. Phillies fans don't seem to care. They're not about niceties. They're here for the game.

Once we entered the gate, our first goal was to get a Philly Cheesesteak sandwich. Scott dug up some excellent intelligence on the sandwich. If you want to order it like a real Philadelphian, you need to add "Whiz Wit" to your order. That gets you the sandwich with Cheez Whiz and fried onions. It was amazing.

So was the game. The Phillies won 11-7.

Scott and I had one more goal. Alan Trammell, the Tigers 1984 World Series MVP, was a coach with the Cubs. My brother Scott, who worked at "The Toronto Star," and I were trying to meet him. Scott had called the Cubs, not on behalf of the newspaper, but without keeping his media credentials a secret, either. He asked if we could have lunch with Tram or buy him a drink. The Cubs were nice, but declined. They did tell Scott, "We love Tram." Who wouldn't?

After the game, Scott and I went down beside the Cubs dugout and called for Trammell, but that didn't work either. That meeting remains on our bucket list.

Before we left, I put a picture of Dave in another planter.

We had rooms in the only hotel in the stadium parking lot complex, so we headed to the hotel bar. Well, not all of us. Scott spent the entire night on the phone with a woman he'd started dating. He'd been divorced for three years and had dated, but not without heartache. I hoped the woman on the other end of the line was worth missing out on quality guy time.

On the way home, we stopped at the Baseball Hall of Fame. I hid a picture of Dave behind the Cal Ripken exhibit. The Orioles' legend was going to be inducted into the Hall later that summer.

I wish the guys from Thunder Bay had joined us, but we all had to deal with Dave's death in our own way. I still can't decide whether this trip made me miss Dave less. I certainly couldn't miss him more.

Toronto Blue Jays— Alternate

Style: structured, fitted
Made by New Era, 5950
Bought at Rogers Centre in the mid-2000s

For some reason, the Blue Jays changed their colors to black, with a little blue in 2004. It was a terrible decision and completely out of character for the organization.

The team has never thrown money around recklessly but will splurge when they have a chance to win. When they make a big spend, the Blue Jays get the most out of it. The Jays still play in the first MLB stadium with a retractable roof, even though it's outdated and outclassed by every stadium since Camden Yards showed the way.

If the Blue Jays were a person, you'd trust them to do your taxes. That's why the move to black felt so wrong. Toronto already had perfectly good uniforms with perfectly good colors. Why mess with that? And, no, wearing black didn't make them look cool. It made them look like they were trying too hard.

I hated the scheme and the hats, except for this variant they adapted a few years later. I like the silver lettering and the T. After all, Toronto was my home.

I'd come to appreciate the Jays more now that I was a parent. Shane attended his first game when he was five weeks old. Coming to a game with a child is a different experience, something the Jays were aware of. Junior Jays Saturdays were ideal for families. Outside the stadium, kids played in bouncy castles and had their faces painted. Certain seat prices were reduced for children. We liked sitting in leftfield with Shane because there was a play area behind the seats. Shane developed a game day routine. Play outside, then get a slice of pizza and eat that during the first three innings, hang out in the leftfield play area for the middle three innings, then eat a bag of popcorn and watch the last three innings.

After the game, the kids could run the bases. Lines of families descended through the concrete walkways and emerged through the rightfield bullpen onto the turf. When the kids reached first base, they were off. If you were quick, you could get to home plate in time to take a picture of your child finishing the journey. We often would have an usher take a picture of our family on the field. The Jays provided us with a lot of happy memories.

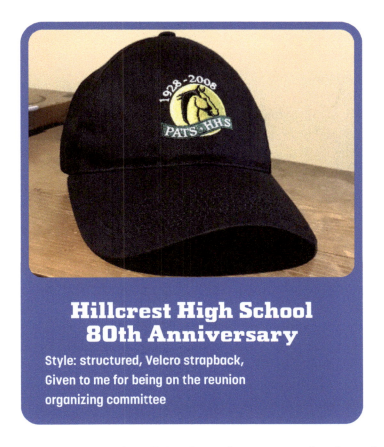

Hillcrest High School 80th Anniversary

Style: structured, Velcro strapback,
Given to me for being on the reunion organizing committee

In 2008, Hillcrest High School was having its eightieth, and final, anniversary. The school was closing, soon to be turned into condos.

Five years earlier, Bonnie Paajanen—a friend's mother who had attended Hillcrest herself—had asked me to help with the school's seventy-fifth anniversary. My job was to set up career day and the alumni football game. I was all over it.

For career day, I skipped the big success stories in favor of people who had struggled to find paths to rewarding careers. Those stories were more inspiring. At the football game, the alumni played the current junior team in touch football. None of the alumni had been a quarterback so I stepped up.

Late in the game, I fired a bullet downfield that hit a receiver in his outstretched hands in full stride. He cruised into the endzone. The crowd roared. I was surprised at the outburst. I felt a warm, glowing rush. I could see how this could go to your head. In fairness, it was a beautiful pass. It was also intended for my friend Dave Mack, whom I'd overthrown by about five yards. I kept that to myself though. No need to diminish the adulation. The alumni won handily.

Because of the football game, I missed a presentation in the auditorium where current drama students read a bit of a valedictory address from each decade. Mine had been chosen to represent the 1980s. I wouldn't have known that if Nancy hadn't been in the auditorium for the presentation. Of course, I was disappointed she didn't see my gridiron glory, but I was happy to know my speech resonated with whomever picked it.

My Blues Brother Dave Hagberg hadn't taken take part in any of the seventy-fifth anniversary events. He should have been all over that party. He was a star in high school, and everyone wanted him at the anniversary. He made excuses. His kids had hockey in the afternoon. That was legitimate, but I couldn't understand why he passed on everything.

I'd organized a small get together at a local pub after the football game for people in our year. When the game ended, I had called Dave and told him he had to come to this. He'd said OK.

Dave had loved seeing everyone. He'd told our friend Michele Morrison he remembered the first time he saw her in high school. "You were wearing a light blue sweater." Michele was moved that she was remembered so vividly, especially by someone as popular as Dave. Dave had recalled off-color stories with other classmates. He had been in his glory, animated and laughing, as I knew he would be.

The next night Dave had come over to my parents' house and told us he'd gone into Hillcrest in the morning and looked at the picture displays in each room. We were together in a lot of them. I'd told Dave I'd been right around the corner in the cafeteria that morning at a pancake breakfast. Why hadn't he come in? Why hadn't he told me he was there? Dave didn't have an answer.

By the fall of 2008, Dave was gone but I felt his shadow all over the eightieth anniversary event. Once again, I organized career day and the football game. My brothers Jim, Scott, and I were all on the field together. That was a first. We just managed a tie with the current team.

Dick Henderson, a former football and basketball coach, saw me in the hallway. Back in high school, Mr. Henderson had asked Dave and me to do announcements for his teams all the time. He greeted me with a big handshake and bigger smile. "We need you to do another announcement! That's what this event needs!"

I replied, "I'd love to but we're a man down for that job."

Mr. Henderson's smile faded, and he looked off into the distance. I don't remember what he said, but I won't forget his reassuring pat on my shoulder. He missed Dave, too.

Detroit Red Wings 2008 Stanley Cup Champions

Style: structured, flexfit
Made by Reebok
Bought online after the Red Wings won the Cup

I thought the Red Wings' Stanley Cup victories were over when Steve Yzerman, my favorite hockey player ever, retired in 2006. I should not have underestimated them.

Just two years later, in 2008, the Wings beat the Penguins in six games, earning the right to hoist Lord Stanley's chalice for the fourth time in eleven years. In true Red Wings fashion, Steve Yzerman said this was the Red Wings' best championship team. Always classy.

This hat has a mesh back, which I usually don't like, but the material is soft so it's super comfortable. I love the Stanley Cup under the brim.

It was wonderful to see the Wings hoist the Cup again, but a little more than three weeks later, something even better happened. My second son, Curtis, was born on June 30.

It was a Monday, and I was getting ready to go to the office. The next day was Canada Day, so all my colleagues had taken the day off to get a four-day weekend. I'd be alone, so I was wearing a light Detroit Tigers batting practice jersey. Nancy said, "Can you wait a little while before you go to work?"

I smiled. "You bet I can."

We called my brother Scott to take care of Shane then we headed to the hospital. The nurses examined Nancy at about 11:30 a.m. They said Nancy wasn't nearly dilated enough, so it was best to go home. We said we'd hang around for a while. They said, "Fine." No, we didn't need to bring in the bag we'd packed. There was no way we'd need it. The nurses were pretty smug.

Nancy and I ate some lunch then started walking. At 2:30 p.m., Nancy was in a lot of pain, so we went back to the nursing station. The nurses paid us no mind. I'm no medical expert, but the contractions were really close together. Nancy needed attention and wasn't getting it.

I pulled back the curtain around the bed and said to the medical staff, "You need to get in here."

A nurse sauntered in with an orderly. They checked Nancy. The nurse's eyes bulged. "When you were in here last you were one centimeter dilated. Now you're five centimeters dilated."

The orderly stiffened. "I can run this bed to the delivery room. I've done it before."

A few seconds later, we were racing down the hall. The delivery room filled with doctors and nurses the moment we arrived. Just as quickly, they were gone. I was alone in the room with Nancy, who was deep into contractions.

I thought, *Am I going to have to deliver this baby myself inside the hospital?*

Then I thought, *I really, really need to go to the bathroom.*

This needed to be addressed. I couldn't soil myself while delivering my next child.

When Nancy's contraction stopped, I said, "Nancy, I really hate to tell you this, but I NEED to go to the bathroom now. I promise I'll be back before the next contraction."

I dashed ten feet to the bathroom, whizzed for all I was worth, and was back in under a minute. Yes, I washed my hands. Fortunately, the medical team arrived when I did. Two crises averted.

I told the doctor that we'd asked for an epidural. He replied, "We won't have time for that."

I looked down and saw the baby crowning. Unlike Shane's birth, which was like a horror movie for me, I suddenly felt light, almost euphoric.

"Nancy, he's almost here!"

"Just give him a push," the doctor said.

Nancy bore down once and out came Curtis. We had already named him. I laughed. He was squashed and beautiful. The nurses cleaned him off and put him on Nancy's chest. It was 3:07 p.m.

I tell the boys that Shane started our family and Curtis completed it. That's exactly how it felt in that moment. The family felt whole.

The next day, Scott showed up with Shane. The first thing Shane said to his little brother was, "Do you want a Chicken McNugget?" They've been the best of brothers ever since.

New York Mets—Alternate
Style: structured, fitted
Made by New Era, 5950
Bought at the Blue Jays Gift Shop New Era 5950 sale

Right before Dave died, he sent me an e-mail telling me how much he wanted to take Ryan to Yankee Stadium before it closed at the end of the 2008 season. Ryan loved baseball and was a huge Yankees fan.

After we lost Dave, I swore I would get his family to Yankee Stadium. So, I organized one last big baseball trip in 2008 to make it happen. I pitched the trip to Relita, and she signed off on it. So did my wife Nancy, who agreed to let me go while she stayed home alone with an infant and a four-year-old. It was a gigantic ask, but she knew what the trip meant. Nancy is the best person I have ever met.

We picked a time when the Mets and Yankees were both home. This was also the last year for Shea Stadium, the Mets ballpark.

Four people agreed to go with us. Larry flew down separately with his father. Reynaldo, Relita's brother, joined us. Chris Blow, who had joined us on the last year's trip, came with us, too. Both Larry and Chris knew how loaded this situation was, but Larry was a close friend who had met Dave. Not so with Chris, who was just an acquaintance. Still, Chris rode in the van with Relita, Ryan, Ben, Reynaldo, and me. He was in the thick of it.

Here's what you need to know about Chris. He's six feet four inches, athletic, with a scraggly beard and red hair. Chris has an artist's soul and the easy disposition of everyone's little brother. He approaches life with an open heart. From the minute we picked up Chris, he was involved in every conversation. It's like we had all known him forever.

We drove down in one day, then had a day in New York before catching the subway up to Queens to watch a night game—the Mets playing the Astros. Relita, Ryan, Ben, Reynaldo, and I were taking a hop-on-hop-off bus to check out the city. Larry and his dad had their own plans.

Chris was going for a run in Central Park. He'd forgotten his running shorts at home, so he bought some I Heart New York boxer shorts. Chris would be going running in the boxers and a blue University of Kentucky basketball jersey. He must have tucked his room key in his sock because he didn't have pockets. He looked so odd I took a picture of him before we left. We agreed to meet at 4 p.m., to catch the train to the Mets game.

We all went our separate ways, then returned to the hotel lobby. Everyone was there except Chris. After fifteen minutes, I was getting worried. Chris wasn't answering his phone. We couldn't reach him. Our friend was out there alone in New York City, with no identification, strangely dressed.

At 4:30 p.m., we started planning search options. Where was the nearest police station? We saw one in Times Square. How long does someone have to be missing before you report them? I was getting ready to give everyone their tickets and go show the police my picture of Chris in his new boxers.

Then Chris showed up. What the hell happened?

He'd run to the park, found a nice spot on the grass to watch girls, and fallen asleep. It was quite an image, this giant ginger, asleep in the park in his boxers. Chris shrugged, then we took the long subway ride to Shea Stadium in Queens for the game.

The Mets destroyed the Astros 9-1. Carlos Delgado hit two home runs. I hid a picture of Dave under the electrical wires in the steel girders just above our heads in the 200-level. Dave would have liked that.

After the game we took the subway back to the hotel, exiting at Times Square. When we walked out into the lights, eleven-year-old Ben's eyes bulged. He was entranced by this electric world. Dave would have liked that, too.

I like this Mets hat, even though I disapproved of the Mets black uniforms. On the cap, the blue and black contrast nicely and there is a tasteful amount of orange. If the Mets had used black just for alternate uniforms, I would have been OK with that, primarily because it gave us this sharp-looking cap.

New York Yankees

Style: structured, fitted
Made by New Era, 5950
Bought at Yankee Stadium in 2008

The trip to see the Mets at Shea Stadium was fun, but the main event was seeing Ryan's beloved Yankees play at Yankee Stadium. I was ready to deliver Dave's family to Yankee Stadium and fulfil my best friend's wish.

I had the logistics all planned out. I'd built in a little time for missed trains, but not much. I hadn't accounted for a thirteen-year-old boy who had to go to the bathroom. Right as we were about to leave, Relita told me the news. Ryan added the kicker: "I don't like to be rushed." I'm not known for my patience, and I felt everyone's eyes on me.

Ryan and I looked at each other. Ryan was a huge Yankees fan, but when you've got to go you've got to go. "You've got fifteen minutes," I said. Ryan smiled and left for his mission.

Ryan made his deadline, and we were on the No. 4 north, just slightly behind schedule.

We got to the centerfield bleacher entrance close to game time. Relita almost fought off a security guard who held her up while her kids raced on ahead. Still, we'd made it. We were in our bench seats for the introductions.

This was exactly what Dave wanted. I felt like I had kept a deathbed promise to my best friend. I'd brought his family to Yankee Stadium before the wrecking ball claimed it. Sitting in the warm evening air with the magnificence of one of baseball's true cathedrals stretched out in front of me, tears welled in my eyes. I tucked a picture of Dave under my seat.

After the game, we walked behind the Yankees bullpen. I yelled down to the grounds crew. One of the guys looked up. I waved a plastic baggie. He knew what I wanted. He nodded, then I dropped the bag to him, and he filled it with dirt from the bullpen mound. Then he threw it to me. Some jerk tried to intercept the toss but missed. What a score. We had Yankee Stadium dirt.

As for the game, Alex Rodriguez, the Yankees' best player, went 0-5 with an error, two strikeouts and hit into two double plays in a 7-3 loss to the Red Sox, their archrivals. If A-Rod had even an average game, the Yankees would have won.

At breakfast the next day, I mentioned to Yankees fan Ryan that Rodriguez probably had his worst game ever and read him the stats. Ryan looked at me and said, "And we were there to see it."

Detroit Lions
Style: structured, Velcro strapback
Bought at Ford Field in 2008

The trip to New York City had exhausted all the funds in my goodwill bank at home. I was preparing for domestic autumn with my young family when Nancy told me she wanted to go home for a week with Shane and baby Curtis to see her mom and sister. She was on maternity leave, so why not? I still had to work, but being a supportive husband, I told her she had my full support. I swear that it only occurred to me afterward that I had a weekend in October to myself. What to do?

I checked the NFL and NCAA football schedules. The Steelers were on the road, but the Michigan Wolverines were hosting the Illinois Fighting Illini and the Detroit Lions were hosting the Chicago Bears.

When I mentioned my plans to my brother Scott and my parents, they decided to join me. Scott's new girlfriend Natasha, the recipient of the Famous Philadelphia Phone Call, was coming, too.

I hadn't been to Michigan's legendary stadium, the Big House, which holds more than 100,000 fans, since I lived in Ann Arbor as a young boy. The Wolverines are usually a powerhouse, but they fielded the worst team they had in decades and were kicked by Illinois. It was disappointing. The experience at the Lions game, however, was expected.

The Detroit Lions make a lot of bad decisions. Ford Field is one. This was my first time at the new stadium, which opened in 2002. Like so much with the Lions, a team with gorgeous silver and Honolulu blue uniforms, the stadium is superficially beautiful. The former Hudson's department store warehouse is incorporated—inside and outside—on the south side, its lovely brick exposed. Frosted skylights provide natural light to the field and concourse. The corridors are spacious, and, with just 65,000 seats, you feel close to the game. It's like a playing field inside a stylish mall.

However, there are two major problems with Ford Field. First, the field is artificial turf. The plastic grass has improved from its early days as fuzzy concrete that shortened players' careers, but it's still a far cry from the natural grass. This field was made from Firestone tires, recalled because it was believed they led to the death of hundreds of drivers. The Lions were literally playing on a field made from failure.

Second, Ford Field has a roof, making it cozy warm for the fans but giving away a huge advantage for a northern team hosting southern teams late in the season. In the winter, the Steelers, Green Bay Packers, and New York Giants play outdoors. They also win. The Lions took the comfortable way out instead of looking for a competitive edge.

At the time we saw the game, the Lions had just fired Matt Millen, a former player and broadcaster. Millen must have talked a good game to Lions owner, William Clay Ford, Sr., because in 2001, Ford hired Millen as the president and chief executive officer, despite his complete lack of experience in the front office. Millen even told Ford he wasn't qualified.

Ford replied, "You'll figure it out." He didn't.

Millen turned the Lions from a borderline playoff team to one of the most pathetic franchises in sports history. The Lions averaged four wins a season and went three years without winning a road game. For doing such a terrible job, Ford made Millen the second-highest-paid general manager in the NFL.

That reign ended days before we took our seats to see the Lions play the Bears. The losing, however, didn't.

The Bears crushed the Lions 34-7. It was the Lions' 51st consecutive sellout, despite losing all their games so far that year. No biggie, they lost the rest of their games that season, too, becoming the first NFL team to go 0-16.

We walked out of the stadium in our Lions gear, five long faces in a sea of dejected Detroit fans. A guy in a Bears jersey, drinking a beer and smiling, said to us, "It's going to be all right, Detroit. It's going to be all right."

I would have known he was a Bears fan even without the jersey. That's not something any Lions fan would ever say.

Go Lions!

Toronto Raptors
Style: structured, flexfit
Made by Adidas
Bought in the mid-2000s

For a couple of years, I shared season's tickets with a few people. I had tickets for about seven games a year. Sunday games were my favorite because I could bring Shane.

Our seats were in the upper level, beside the aisle where announcers did standups for the in-game broadcast. Consequently, Shane got on the big screen a lot. He was a super-cute four-year-old and was always decked out in Raptors gear.

One Sunday for a game against the New York Knicks, Shane and I arrived early, both wearing red Chris Bosh jerseys and Raptors hats. Shane was eating a bag of popcorn the size of his torso as we watched the warmups. We were the only ones in the section. A well-dressed young man wearing a headset approached us.

"My name is Luka. I work for the Raptors," he said. "You look like big fans."

I assured him that we were.

"How would you like to see the game a little closer?" he asked.

I assured him that we would.

Out of our seats and down the stairs we went. Luka asked Shane who his favorite player was.

"Chris Bosh," Shane answered.

Down and down, we went.

"We like to find parents and children who look like big fans and upgrade them. But we need you to go crazy, make a lot of noise."

I assured him that we would.

Luka led us to the 100 level, along the baseline of the court. We turned left onto the hardwood, just beside the basket, and he said, "These are your seats."

We were in the first row. Our feet were on the court.

I looked Luka in the eyes, shook his hand and said, "Thank you so much. We really appreciate this."

Luka handed me the tickets for the seats. The face value was $1,041 each. The pair cost more than our last vacation.

Chris Bosh towered over us, taking shots in the warmup. The Raptors mascot was a few feet away. This was great! Shane was elbow deep in popcorn when the Raptor high-fived him. I took out my camera and called the Raptor back. The mascot sat down next to Shane and started in on his popcorn. Shane howled with laughter. I took a few pictures.

The afternoon was a sports fan's dream, more for me than my four-year-old son. At one point, Shane asked, "Why aren't we in our seats?"

I replied, "Would you rather sit way up there?"

He said, "Yes."

He even asked to leave early because he was bored.

"We're not going anywhere," I replied.

Late in the fourth quarter during a boisterous time-out, I put Shane in my hands and bounced him above my head. He was laughing and waving. Suddenly, Shane was on the Jumbotron, bigger than life.

The Raptors beat the Knicks 111-110.

The next day, Shane wore his Raptors jersey to daycare. He ran straight to his daycare worker and exclaimed: "I went to the Raptors game yesterday! Our feet were on the court! The Raptor ate my popcorn!" He said all of this as one word.

At the end of the week, he brought the picture of the Raptor eating his popcorn for show and tell.

A month later, Curtis saw his first game. The whole family watched the Raptors play the Jazz from the loud Sprite Zone cheap seats. Curtis squirmed in my lap as I held ear plugs in place. No upgrade for that game, but we were still all geared up and together, cheering on our Raptors.

I wore this hat to both games. The basketball claw is my favorite Raptor logo, and I prefer this curved brim. The crown has a low profile, so the structured front doesn't look too boxy. Great hat.

Detroit Tigers
Style: unstructured, fullback, size L
Made by '47 Brand

The Tigers were in town to play the Jays in early April 2009, so I bought seats above the visitors' dugout for the whole family. This was a special game.

Two rookies named Ricky, both former first-round draft picks, were starting for each team. Ricky Romero started for the Jays and Ricky Porcello for the Tigers.

Porcello's family was a row in front of us and off to our right. I didn't need to ask if they were related. They were all wearing Tigers road jerseys with Porcello's name and number on the back. At that point in his career, the only other person who had a jersey like that would have been Ricky Porcello himself.

It was also special because this was Curtis's first baseball game. Both Curtis and Shane wore Tigers gear. Nancy's a Blue Jays fan, so I must have rushed to dress them first. Like any good sports fan parent, I try my best to indoctrinate my children into supporting my favorite teams. It starts with gear. Both boys have had Tigers', Steelers', and Raptors' clothing since birth.

In fact, when I sent my family the first picture of Curtis, Jim replied, "Why isn't he wearing Tigers clothes? He's hours old! You're dropping the ball, Craig."

I put a Tigers shirt on Curtis immediately.

The indoctrination doesn't always take, but you have to do your best. If they pick another team, you just hope it isn't the Dallas Cowboys.

Romero topped Porcello that day, but Curtis wouldn't wait long for another shot at a Tigers victory. We were in Comerica Park a month later to see the Tigers play Oakland. Our seats were about a third of the way up above first base. Nancy dressed Curtis in a green-and-blue striped long-sleeve shirt with a wide-brimmed floppy hat to protect him from the sun.

I made sure he was wearing a Tigers bib. I also bought him a little stuffed Tiger. Unfortunately, I forgot my camera and my phone didn't have one yet. I talked the girls in front of me into taking a picture of Curtis and me at his first Tigers home game. I gave them our home address. A month later, the pictures arrived in the mail. Thank you, Detroit fans! The Tigers beat the A's 11-7.

I didn't really appreciate some aspects of Comerica Park until I had children. When the park opened, I thought the baseball Ferris wheel and Tigers merry-go-round were gimmicky. When I started taking my kids there, I loved them. Curtis and Shane looked forward to that part of the trip to the park for years.

This style of hat is often referred to as a "dad hat." The name works for me. I love being a dad and how comfortable the '47 Brand hats are. This logo, sometimes called "the surprised Tiger," is a favorite. It feels like youth and good times at the park.

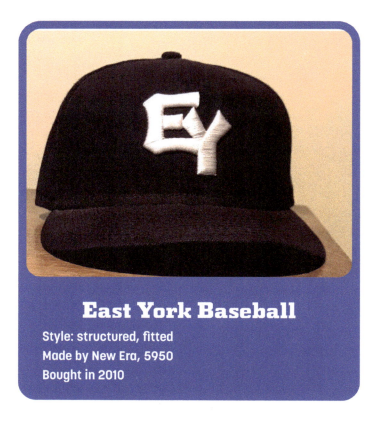

East York Baseball
Style: structured, fitted
Made by New Era, 5950
Bought in 2010

I love baseball but I was too insecure to play in a league as a kid—and the last one chosen when I played at school or with friends. When I started playing softball as a young adult, I read books on batting and fielding and practiced every chance I got.

By the time we enrolled Shane in East York Baseball House League, in 2010, I had the basics down. I started coaching our house-league team the Coyotes, along with another coach. The players were six- and seven-year-olds, the youngest kids at the lowest level. We had cool black uniforms.

A couple of things became clear early on with the Coyotes. No practice time was scheduled, so we had to keep it simple. Also, very few balls were hit in the air. The most important skills the kids could learn was to pick up the ball, throw it to the right base and to catch it.

I used just one drill. I'd roll a ball to a player. The player would pick it up and throw it to another player at a base. A line of players would rotate between the two positions. That's it. Learning these fielding basics was even more important than learning to hit at this stage.

At the plate, players would get five pitches from a machine. If they didn't hit one, the ball was placed on a tee, so the ball would always be put in play. The league had a five-run mercy rule, except for the last inning. Five runs were scored in most innings. If you could get three outs consistently, you'd have a good shot at winning the game.

Our team had fun playing all summer. We kept it light but encouraged the kids to try hard and think about which base to throw to if they got the ball.

The East York Baseball Association finished the season with a single Saturday event in August, where every team played at least one game. The older kids had a playoff, but we had just one game to wrap things up. To this day, the Coyotes' final game was my proudest moment in coaching.

Our players recorded three outs in every inning, and we won. The kids were thrilled. Almost as thrilled as I was.

As a coach, I tried to make the game as inviting as possible for kids who aren't naturals and who give an error too much weight. You shouldn't have to be good at something to enjoy it. There should be joy in playing, in the act of trying. That joy makes you want to play more, which gives you a chance to become good.

One of the worst players I coached loved the game so much, he played all he could, went to every skills clinic, every tryout, and eventually became an AA rep ball player. I'm proud to have been a small contributor to his baseball journey. For me, victory isn't winning the championship. It's having the players I coach come back next season.

When the East York Baseball executive made these New Era 5950 hats available, I bought one right away. Even though I was coaching the youngest kids at the lowest level, wearing the official hat made me feel more connected to the game. I had felt I was missing something by not playing as a child. Now, as a coach, I knew I was contributing. I was part of baseball.

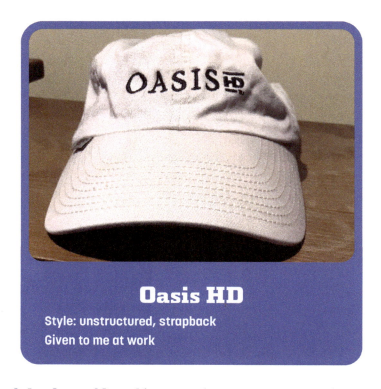

Oasis HD
Style: unstructured, strapback
Given to me at work

One of the downsides of being a television executive is that you don't get to go on cool shoots anymore. The conferences are usually in beautiful locations, and they can be fun, but a great shoot is an adventure.

One of my favorite projects at High Fidelity was working on a series for our Oasis HD channel called "A Park for All Seasons." It was sponsored by Parks Canada, the federal department in charge of Canada's National Parks. Each episode featured a Canadian National Park. Our field crew went to the most beautiful places in Canada, from Quttinirpaaq in the Arctic to Point Pelee at the southernmost point, to Terra Nova on the east coast and Pacific Rim on the west coast. I thought it was the best job in the country. I was jealous.

My boss, John Panikkar, insisted I go on one of the trips to supervise our first 3D shoot. I'm glad he did. The location was Gwaii Haanas National Park Reserve, National Marine Conservation Reserve and Haida Heritage

Site. It's a stunning rainforest 100 kilometers off the British Columbia coast in the southern part of the Haida Gwaii Islands.

Getting to the island from Vancouver was nerve-racking. We had so many bags of gear packed onto the small flight from Vancouver out to the island, that it bumped all the other luggage. That situation was announced to all the passengers when we landed. They glared at us as we picked up our bags. It needed to happen, though. If any of our equipment failed to make the trip, we'd be waiting another day and our carefully planned schedule would be a mess.

To understand the challenges of this shoot, you need to understand the landscape we were facing, and the problems created by shooting in 3D. This format requires a lot of equipment. You need two identical cameras, perfectly calibrated, and distanced from each other. If anything is wrong, looking at the 3D image will give the viewer a headache. To get the foreground and background movement that are essential in 3D, we put the camera on a jib—a big arm that goes up and down and moves side to side. Every time you move to a different location, you tear down gear, move it, and build it again. In short, shooting in 3D takes more equipment, and more time, so you come home with way less material.

There was another complication. Since the park is on an island, you can only travel around by boat or airplane. We rented a boat and loaded it up with our gear, our six-person crew, and a park ranger. Because of the huge tidal swings, the boat couldn't get too close to shore. So, we had an inflatable Zodiac to get the gear from boat to shore.

Every day we'd load a ton and a half of gear into the Zodiac, make multiple trips to shore, and haul the heavy equipment up rock beaches at low tide to set up. At night, we'd tear down, haul everything back to the Zodiac, then load the gear back on the boat. What didn't fit inside was strapped outside on deck.

On top of that, we were shooting in a rainforest. That name isn't an accident. One day we shot in a downpour under the forest canopy. Even under the cover of huge trees, it was like working in a shower. When we finished, our boat was gone. We thought we were abandoned for some tense minutes until the Zodiac showed up. The captain had to navigate a difficult path between the rocks before the tide went any lower.

It was all worth it. The island is stunning. Majestic Sitka spruce towered over us, and green moss lay at our feet. Standing in this beauty, it was easy to see why so much of Indigenous spirituality is inspired by nature. How could living here not inform every aspect of your life? The highlight was seeing the totem poles carved by the Haida at SGang Gwaay. The Haida don't restore these stunning pieces of art. The poles return to the land when they've run their course.

The shoot was challenging, but one of the highlights of my career. I brought these hats for the crew and people participating in the shoot. I learned back in my days at TSN that people love getting a free hat. It creates incredible goodwill. Million-dollar athletes break into a smile when you give them this small gift. I wore this hat every day on the Gwaii Haanas shoot, and I'll never give it up.

radX
Style: unstructured, strapback
Given to me at work

radX was our adventure channel at High Fidelity HDTV. I appeared on the channel on a regular basis because of one of my hobbies.

In spring 2010, my younger brother Scott and I got an email from our older brother Jim with a link to a Tough Mudder, a new event taking place in New Jersey in November—a week after Jim's birthday and not far from his house. Tough Mudder was a ten-mile obstacle course through mud on a dirt-bike track site with challenges like running through fire, then jumping into an ice-cold lake and swimming across it. The event looked insane.

I had no idea if I could do it. So, I was in. I needed a challenge, especially something physical. Scott was in, too. My Texas SWAT team cousin Lou and his nephew Michael also signed up. So did my friend Larry.

This was just the third Tough Mudder event ever. All of us were concerned about getting hypothermia during the swim across the lake. We weren't alone. My Dad was mad at us for considering doing something so potentially dangerous. Nancy agreed with him. Their disapproval only made the event more enticing.

We trained like hell. We needed to. Other than Michael, we were not young. Jim would be fifty, I was forty-seven, Larry, forty-six, Scott, forty-five, Lou in his early forties and Michael his early thirties. Jim sent us a half-marathon training schedule, which I added to the weightlifting program I was on, Turbulence Training. Jim, Scott, Larry, and I shared our progress. Lou and Michael seemed less intense than the rest of us. Still when the big day arrived, we all looked to be in good shape and ready to go.

Shane and Curtis, just six and two years old, were too young to stand out in the November cold all day, so they stayed home with Nancy. It had been two years since my last sports trip away from the family, so my absence wasn't an issue. The rest of the clan came down to New Jersey: Mom, Dad, Scott's girlfriend Natasha, and Jim's daughter, my nineteen-year-old niece Danielle—who was in her first year at McGill. Jim's in-laws—Lynn's sister Mary Jane and her husband Scott Gordon—also made the trek down from Canada.

This adventure would be well documented. Scott brought his own camera and my nephew—Jim's seventeen-year-old son Mitch—agreed to use mine. Lynn's friend, a photographer, volunteered to take more shots.

Because looking like a team makes you feel like a team, I had shirts made with our group's name on the front, "The Dirty Old Men." Debates on the types of shirts we should wear were detailed and without consensus. Most of us agreed to skintight tech shirts that would dry quickly and wouldn't chafe our nipples. Some shirts had short sleeves, some long. On race day, Scott and Lou covered their shirts with another shirt. We didn't match completely, but we were a team.

It was sunny and cold when the event started. A monster truck led us out from the start line. We jogged behind it. Tough Mudder is not a race. They don't time you. The real beauty of the event is the expectation that you'll help your fellow Tough Mudders through the course.

The third obstacle was the one we dreaded the most, Walk the Plank. You climb a rope up to a 15-foot platform, then jump into the lake, which was almost cold enough to freeze over at the time. Then you had to swim half the length of a football field across the lake and go under three barrels. It was about one mile into the ten-mile race. This would make or break us.

The crowd hit a bottleneck at the bottom of the platform. Once we got to the front of the line, we climbed the ropes and assembled at the top. Below us inky black water beckoned. There wasn't much time to worry. As soon as the people in front of us were clear Jim jumped in. Larry and I went right after him.

I plunged into the lake. The cold hit me like a punch in the stomach. My body seized up as I went deep into dark and cold. Parts of my body that were on my outside felt like they retreated to my insides. After a moment immobilized in a weightless chill, I kicked for the surface. My face broke through the water, and I gasped. I had to get out of there.

As I swam across the water, I thought, *If there's a lineup at those barrels, I won't be waiting politely.* Fortunately, the path was clear. After ducking under all three barrels. I trudged through the muddy shore onto the beach. I could see my mom and dad with the cheering section.

Jim, Larry, and I walked over to them, then looked back. Scott, Lou, and Michael were way behind us. When they finally arrived, they told us someone jumped in before them and came up sputtering and flailing. The hapless swimmer was going to drown. Military volunteers pulled him out of the lake.

That sight reminded us that there was an element of danger in the event. Still, when we got out of the lake, everyone felt great! We weren't going to get hypothermia! The butterflies disappeared and we were off and running. One obstacle had us climb over rolling mounds, where viscous mud seeped into our shoes, shirts, and even our shorts. Then we slid into watery trenches, which washed the goop away. On the dirt bike track, we had to run up a muddy hill. Everyone reached the top except me because I had picked street running shoes instead of trail footwear. We climbed over ten-foot walls, through huge drainpipes, and under cargo nets. Midway through, Jim grabbed two handfuls of mud and rubbed them into my hair. All the while we laughed like children splashing in puddles. We had a blast. Dad even enjoyed watching us play. He called Nancy and told her there was nothing to worry about.

The Dirty Old Men crossed the finish line together, collected our event T-shirts, and went back to Jim's place for showers and Jim's birthday party, beautifully catered by Lynn. She can really throw a party. We watched the pictures and videos of our exploits, showed off our scrapes and bruises, and basked in our accomplishment.

There was one more order of business. Tough Mudder offered a free tattoo or a shaved head for people who completed the event. They were also fundraising for Wounded Warrior, which supports soldiers maimed in war. I took pledges and said that if I raised $1,000, I'd have my head shaved. My total was $1,595, which punched my ticket to baldness. No one was shaving heads at the finish line, so Mitch stepped up at the party. He shaved Michael's head, then mine. We paused for a few pictures, then Mitch finished the job.

This was one of the best days of my life. Moments of glorious conquest are best when shared. My brothers and I didn't get much time together and this day bridged gaps of time and distance. Each of us likes a challenge, so athletics had always been common ground.

Our parents had always been supportive and felt ownership in our achievements. Our sports trophies are still on display in my parents' family room, including my dad's favorites—the three patches Scott, Jim, and I had received after being selected by the Hillcrest coaching staff to attend an athletic leadership camp. Having our parents watch us strive and overcome was both familiar and reassuring.

Having extended family in Lou and Michael there made it even better. The same for Larry, who was no longer just my pal. He was a friend of the family. Top that off with an evening of revelry to mark the occasion and you have a milestone day in your life. I suspect a picture from this day will be on display at each of our funerals.

I wanted to do it again. The next Tough Mudder was in April on a ski hill in Pennsylvania. Michael was the only Dirty Old Man who wanted to take part, but his wife Katy was game. So, the three of us signed up. At work, after hearing my tales of glory, the team in charge of short-form content for radX decided this would make a nice item, especially since it happened to be on the way to another shoot.

In April, Michael, Katy, and I ran up and down a ski hill through an even tougher obstacle course than we'd faced in New Jersey. I wore a camera mounted to a hockey helmet. Katy was the focus of the story since it was her first time. We wore radX shirts and I got this hat.

I did seven Tough Mudders over five years. I loved them. Eventually, I got bored, my knees got sore, and I ran out of partners. It was glorious fun while it lasted though.

I also like this hat and its classic X-Men vibe.

Pittsburgh Steelers
Style: unstructured, snapback
Made by '47 Brand

In late November 2010, the Steelers were playing the Bills in Buffalo. I wasn't going to miss the chance to see the Steelers when they were just an hour and a half away, but I wondered about bringing the kids. It wasn't just that the game was outside in November. We could bundle them up for a few hours. Football games tend to be gladiatorial, and not just on the field.

I loved going to games in Buffalo with the TSN crew. We'd rent a bus, drink on the way down, and pull out the barbecue once we arrived. Tailgate parties were everywhere in the huge parking lot around Rich Stadium. It was part of the culture. We'd drink some more, along with everyone else who was there early, then head into the game. The fans were usually worked up and lubricated by kickoff, priming them to be both loud and profane. The extent of the testosterone-drenched vitriol varies from fan base to fan base. My brother Jim, who lived in New Jersey, would take his kids to New York Giants games, but not New York Jets games.

Bills fans are passionate but can be a little raucous in the stands. Nancy—a Bills fan herself—and I talked about bringing our boys. We decided two-year-old Curtis was still too young, but Shane, six, was good to go. We arranged for a babysitter, and I bought seats near the front of the upper deck in the end zone.

I had yet to see the Steelers win in person and, with the Bills 2-8 and the Steelers 7-3, this seemed like my chance. When we arrived, our section was fully engaged, but not drunk and rowdy. At least half of them were wearing black and gold, including Shane and me, with our matching Steelers #43 Troy Polamalu road jerseys. Nancy—who wore a blue Buffalo Bills #51 Paul Posluszny jersey—found the Steelers fans obnoxious, but mostly because there were so many of them at her favorite team's home game.

The game went to overtime. Bills' receiver Stevie Johnson was cruising underneath a pass in the end zone right in front of us. And . . . it went through his hands. A few minutes later, Shaun Suisham kicked a forty-one-yard field goal to give the Steelers the win.

Shane and I were thrilled. Nancy, not so much. I was a little worried about how Shane would handle the game, but he had a good time and was super, super cute. Go Steelers!

This is the first unstructured Steelers hat I bought, so I'd have one I could throw in a suitcase or overnight bag. I also like the ragged patch and contrasting stitching. It feels casual and old school.

Detroit Tigers—Road
Style: structured, fitted
Made by New Era, 5950

The first Saturday of every May is Free Comic Book Day. Comic bookstores give away free comic books, created by companies like Marvel and DC.

We'd discovered Free Comic Book Day in 2010 with our friend Melissa, and her son Ethan, who was Shane's age, and it immediately became a family tradition. Shane, Curtis, and Ethan were dressed as Spider-Man, Wolverine, and Batman respectively when we set out for our local comic bookstore, Comics 'N More. The owner, a large, reserved, well-spoken man in his thirties, made an event of the day. In addition to the Free Comic Book Day special issues, he packaged surplus stock into gift bags aimed at different demographics. Nancy's bag contained a "Sense and Sensibility" comic book. The owner took pictures of the boys for the store's website.

After shopping, Shane and Ethan hopped in the back seat of our van, ripped into their gift bags and pulled out trading cards, tiny action figures and lots of comics.

Ethan exclaimed, "Shane! This is the best day of our lives!"

That's the moment Free Comic Book Day became a red-letter day on our calendar.

In 2011, we were all back, joined by Shane's friend Tariq. After a morning of costumes and comics, we had another exciting event. The Tigers were in town to play the Blue Jays and Tigers' superstar pitcher Justin Verlander was pitching. My turn to dress up! I put on my Tigers road hat and jersey, and jacket. The kids traded their costumes for T-shirts and ball caps. Scott and Natasha—who were now engaged—met us at the Jays game.

Our seats were in the 200 level in centerfield. Curtis was wearing a Blue Jays hat. I guess Nancy was working on her own indoctrination. Shane wore a Blue Jays hat, because his friends Ethan and Tariq were, too, but he considered himself a fan of both teams.

Justin Verlander was on fire, shutting down the Jays with 100 MPH fastballs. Frustrated Toronto fans started booing. Shane's friends were yelling, "Go Jays" and booing the Tigers. I looked over. I could see that Shane was conflicted.

My indoctrination had been thorough. He'd only recently learned that the words to "Take Me Out to the Ball Game" were "root, root, root for the home team" not "root, root, root for the Tigers." But I could see that Shane was feeling the pull of his friends' approval. After a few moments, Shane burst out with a passionate "Go Jays! Boo Tigers!"

Then he looked over at me. Our eyes locked. Shane shrugged and continued cheering with his friends. That was the day Shane asserted his independence. I was proud of him.

In the sixth inning, Shane and his friends wanted to go to the kids' section in the 200 level behind the leftfield seats. Nancy and Melissa went with them to supervise. Usually, I'd offer to go, or come later to spell them off. Not today.

Justin Verlander had a perfect game going into the eighth inning. I'd never seen a perfect game, or a no-hitter. The Tigers' best pitcher in a generation was dominating a weak line-up and I was watching it with my brother and fellow Tigers fan. This was perfect. I cheered for every out. Jays' fans started throwing popcorn and candy at me.

Tensions were running high in the eighth inning. Verlander got the first out. Five more to go for a perfect game. Then Verlander walked the catcher, JP Arencebia. The perfect game was over, but the no-hitter was intact. The next batter grounded into a double play to end the inning. Verlander was still topping 100 MPH on the radar gun! We were witnessing brilliance.

The kids were back for the bottom of the ninth. I was happy they were there to witness history.

The first batter popped out. The second batter grounded out. And just like you wished it would happen, the last batter struck out. Justin Verlander had pitched the seventh no-hitter in Tigers history!

The Blue Jays fans, including Nancy, Melissa, Shane, and his friends, were sad. I tried not to gloat, but I doubt I was successful. This was one of the greatest games I'd ever attended.

Man, I love the Detroit Tigers.

Detroit Tigers
Style: unstructured, strapback

Chris Blow invited me to see the Tigers play the Yankees in Detroit in Game 3 of the American League Division Series in 2011. We were joined by his childhood friend, Ed Ward, a huge Tigers fan.

This was another chance to see my all-time favorite Tigers' pitcher Justin Verlander, who was on his way to winning the Cy Young Award and American League MVP that year. JV was brilliant again, as the Tigers beat the Yankees 5-4 to take a 2-1 lead in a series they would eventually win.

However, even better was the pilgrimage we made before the game. Tiger Stadium had been torn down and the field claimed by weeds. A group of Tigers fans couldn't stand to look at it, so they jumped the fence, cut the weeds and started taking care of the field. At first, the police chased them off, but eventually the law relented.

Every weekend, the Navin Field Grounds Crew, using a former name of the stadium that once stood there, would tend this hallowed ground. Chris,

Ed, and I brought a baseball and our gloves and went to the field before the game.

I'd been to the corner of Michigan and Trumbull many times but being here like this was a little unsettling. The stadium was gone, but the field was intact. My mind tried to fill in the grandstand, as I stepped past the outline of the dugout and onto the field.

I looked to my left. Lou Gehrig had sat there, a towel over his head to hide his tears, as his consecutive games streak ended. I looked at the mound. Denny McLain had stood there when he won thirty games in 1968, the last pitcher to do so. I looked to my right. Al Kaline had earned his way into the Hall of Fame out there in rightfield. Straight ahead of me was second base, where Alan Trammell and Lou Whitaker spent more time turning two than any double play combo in baseball history. I walked over to the batter's box. Ty Cobb, Babe Ruth, Ted Williams, Ken Griffey Jr. and Hank Greenberg had stood right here.

It felt like I shouldn't be on this field. This space was for the players. You had to earn your way onto this grass and dirt. I was an intruder. But I was in no hurry to leave. We threw the baseball, took pictures, and soaked in the majesty and history of this now-abandoned field.

I brought Shane and Curtis there the next year. The Navin Field Grounds Crew were excavating the mound. Pitching rubbers, made of wood, that must have dated back a hundred years, were unearthed. Jason Roche was recording it on a small video recorder for a documentary about the Crew, "Stealing Home." Shane, Curtis, and I made the final cut. Jason and I would later become Facebook friends. It's an honor to be part of his document of an important part of Tigers' history and sports fandom.

If I had lived close enough to join the Navin Field Grounds Crew on their Sunday expeditions, I would have worn this hat. The orange suggests construction work or manual labor. The hat is bright and light, perfect for being outdoors in the summer. I also like that it's a reversal of the Tigers' road hat, with a blue D and an orange base. An orange hat is a good thing if you need to be picked out in a crowd.

Detroit Tigers—1983 Road
Style: structured, fitted
Made by American Needle

In March 2012, Nancy, Shane, Curtis, and I took a family vacation to Florida and the Bahamas. Shane was seven and Curtis was three. Doors opened magically wherever we went.

Because Curtis was in a stroller, we were waved to the front of the line while boarding a cruise ship to the Bahamas. On a glass bottom boat, we saw the crew feed Caribbean Reef Sharks. At Universal Studios we were given a private audience with the Marvel Superheroes. Shane was obsessed with alligators and crocodiles, so we went to Gatorland, where we saw a Nile crocodile, an albino gator, and Shane got to sit on an alligator.

The best of the best, though, was in Lakeland, when we saw the Tigers host the Cardinals on St. Patrick's Day at Joker Marchant Stadium. I'd never been to a spring training game and had always dreamed of going.

Exhibition games in every other sport are a drag. You pay full price to see a mix of starters, backups and players who will be cut, in games that don't mean anything. In baseball, it's different.

Maybe it's because the games are played in warm weather locations during February, so they hold the promise of spring. Maybe it's because the game appears to be played at a more relaxed pace. Maybe it's because the stadiums are smaller, more intimate. Whatever the reason, exhibition baseball works.

Shane asked for a green Detroit Tigers hat. Of course, I bought it for him. It was an adult size, but we cinched up the strap in the back. Someday, that hat will be mine.

Our tickets were for general admission seats on the outfield grass, which was awesome. We settled in to relax and catch the game, all geared up in our Tigers clothes. A young woman approached us and said, "Are you a family of four?"

"Why yes we are."

"Would you like better seats?"

"Why, yes we would."

She walked us down the third base side of the stadium, chatting as we headed for our upgrade. Shane was talkative, as usual, and mentioned, "I'm actually a Blue Jays fan. We're from Toronto."

Without missing a beat, our guide said, "Yeah? Have the Blue Jays ever put you behind home plate?"

Shane replied, "Well, no they haven't."

Nancy told Shane, "We're cheering for the Tigers today."

Our guide, true to her word, seated us behind home plate, slightly to the first base side, one row behind and off to the right of the Detroit Tigers President and General Manager, Dave Dombrowski. He'd just spent a lot more of owner Mike Illitch's money bringing free agent first baseman Prince Fielder to Detroit on a nine-year, $214-million contract. I'd admired Dombrowski's work since he created the competitive Expos teams in the 1990s and built the Florida Marlins 1997 championship team. I thought about going over to shake his hand but opted to leave him alone.

It was odd to see both the Tigers and Cardinals wearing Kelly-green jerseys and caps. Still, it was great to be close to so many superstar players.

Miguel Cabrera and Prince Fielder were twenty feet away. Fielder hit the weirdest triple I've ever seen. It bounced between home and first, then sailed over the first baseman's head.

As part of our upgrade, Shane was interviewed by the in-game announcer. Our boy was a natural. We were given gift certificates for a local steak house after the game. Oh yeah, and the Tigers won.

Fantastic vacation.

I didn't buy this hat in Lakeland, but it reminds me of the era when I really started paying attention to all of the Tigers games, even the ones in spring training. It's the type of hat the Tigers wore on the road in the late 1970s and early 1980s.

I love the white outline around the orange D. It makes the D a bit bigger, which I usually don't like, because I think the understated D is more stylish. The bigger D works with the outline though. The white trim makes the orange D stand out from the navy background.

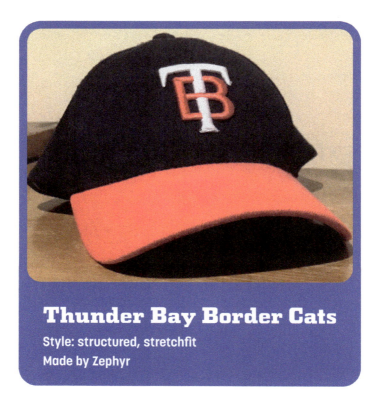

Thunder Bay Border Cats
Style: structured, stretchfit
Made by Zephyr

In the summer of 2012, while I was in Thunder Bay—my parents, Shane, and I went to see the Border Cats, the local team made of collegiate players, play the Alexandria Beetles, up from Minnesota.

In between innings, the Border Cats staged the Subway sandwich races. Two teammates put on huge plastic buns, then one person lies on the ground, while the other races to get plastic tomatoes, meat, and cheese, which they bring back one at a time to throw on the prone teammate. Once all the ingredients for the sandwich are in place, the running bun jumps on the bun on the ground to complete the giant human sandwich.

I'd done it a few years earlier with my friend John Petrynka. Shane thought it was hilarious and was itching to try the sandwich race himself. I flagged down a young woman who was looking for contestants and told her

Shane would be an enthusiastic participant. Shane's eight-year-old exuberance got us in the race.

I would be the prone bun and Shane would gather all the ingredients. They fitted us with bicycle helmets, and we pulled on the plastic buns. Shane's bun went down to his shoe tops. We were competing against two brothers, probably ten or twelve years old.

We took our places and Shane was off, sprinting and smiling down the third-base line, his little feet shuffling frantically. Shane was the first back with the meat. He had a huge lead when he delivered the cheese. On his way back for the tomatoes, the third-base coach for the Beetles, who had been watching the race and smiling, grabbed Shane to slow him down a bit.

It was all in good fun, but it allowed our opponent to overtake Shane. The big plastic tomato landed on me then Shane flopped down to complete the sandwich, but we had lost. The Beetles' third-base coach was laughing in the dugout. He nodded at me as we got up.

What he didn't know was that Shane can be hyper-competitive. This was the kind of loss that could send him into tears. I gave Shane a big hug and laughed. I told him the third-base coach was just playing a joke. The winner was given free Subway sandwiches, but the Border Cats gave us the same prize anyway. Shane embraced the moment, and the joke. It gave him an extra element to the story, which he told to anyone who would listen.

The next day we went to claim our spoils. Since Shane has never liked condiments, or lettuce, or tomatoes, or more than one ingredient on his sandwich, he ordered a bun with cheese slices. Curtis followed his lead. Both boys declared their spartan hoagies delicious and Subway became one of their favorite restaurants.

As for this hat, the Border Cats switched from the cartoonish cat logo to the interlocking TB in 2008. Although I've always liked the charm of the minor league hats' playful logos, I prefer the TB hat for the Border Cats. It feels like it belongs to the city where I grew up more than the cartoon cat ever did.

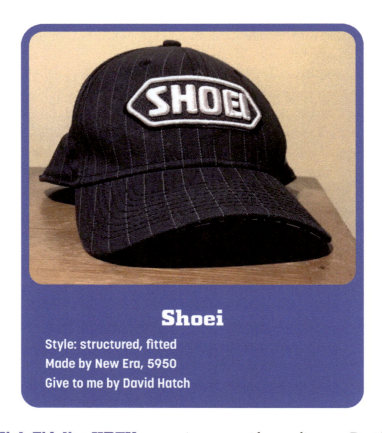

Shoei

Style: structured, fitted
Made by New Era, 5950
Give to me by David Hatch

At High Fidelity HDTV, our primary outside supplier was David and Stacey Hatch's Whistlestop Productions located a couple of hours east of Toronto in Picton, Ontario.

David loves cars and guitars, things I know little about, and we produced series on each that performed well for our niche channels. In time, David and I became friends

Our work lives would change in 2012. Media magnate Michael MacMillan—who'd made a couple of billion dollars selling his previous company Alliance Atlantis—bought my favorite TV home, High Fidelity HDTV, for $85 million.

High Fidelity merged with Glassbox, which ran three TV channels, to create Blue Ant Media. When you pay that kind of money for a company, you get to do what you want with it, and that means putting your people in place. My bosses, John Panikkar and Ken Murphy, had become both wealthy and extraneous. They would no longer be with the company. I kept my job but lost all my authority. Prior to the merger, half the company reported to me. Afterwards, no one did. It was tough to take.

The last show commissioned was "Cities in Blue," a series about how blues developed in different parts of the United States. The project was dreamed up by John, Ken, David, Stacey, and I over dinner in Prince Edward County. All of us loved the blues—David and I had been in bands that played blues, Ken had a collection of tens of thousands of records focusing on 1950s and 1960s artists, John and Stacey were music lovers—so it became a passion project for everyone.

David and I were nominated for a Canadian Screen Award for Writing on the final episode of "Cities in Blue." That seemed to impress some of my new bosses, which helped at work. Mostly, it was nice that the last hurrah of High Fidelity was recognized by our peers. Our small production lost the award to the "Rick Mercer Report," a comedy show on Canada's national broadcaster, the CBC. A team of what appeared to be a dozen writers went on stage to collect the award. Their show was extremely popular and deserved the win. I'm happy with the nomination for our small, obscure production. It meant industry professionals had watched it and thought it was well written.

David, a motorcycle enthusiast, produced a series called "Motorcycle Experience" that has run on TSN for more than thirty years. He gave me this hat by Shoei, a motorcycle helmet-maker. It's a great hat with a clean logo. I love the pinstripes.

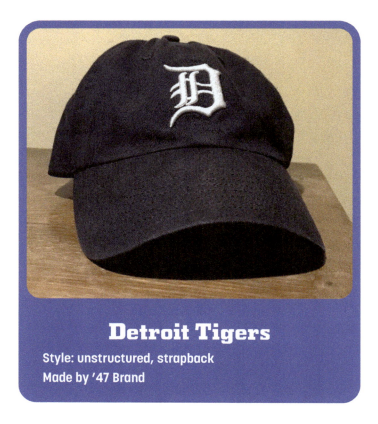

Detroit Tigers
Style: unstructured, strapback
Made by '47 Brand

The Tigers went to the World Series in 2012. I was so excited that I ponied up $500 for an upper deck seat down the third base line for Game Four. That price was far too steep for my Tiger fan friends, let alone my pals who just love baseball, but I couldn't miss the chance to see the Tigers in the World Series. It just doesn't happen that often. I was going to the World Series alone.

Unfortunately, When I rolled into Detroit, the Tigers were down 3-0 to the Giants, it was cold, and a snowstorm was on the way. Tickets were being sold outside for less than face value.

Still, I was pumped. Maybe the Tigers would be the first team to come back from a 3-0 deficit to win the championship. It could happen. My fellow fans did not share my enthusiasm. At one point, late in the game, some guy five rows behind me told me to sit down while I was standing and cheering. I took my seat but come on: This was the World Series!

The Tigers lost in extra innings, and I had to watch the Giants run out on the field to celebrate their second championship in three years. It was depressing. I bought one hat, a World Series hat with both teams' logos, for my cousin Julie who is a fan of both the Giants and the Tigers. I didn't need a hat to remind me of the sweep.

I'm glad I went, though. There are few chances for real success in life and in sports. When they come, you don't want to miss them. At the end of your life, I think these are the things we'll cherish.

This was the last hurrah for these great Tigers clubs of the era. They were the best team in the game for about five years but just couldn't close the deal on a championship. Miguel Cabrera won the triple crown in 2012, leading the league in batting average (.330), home runs (44) and runs batted in (139), the first time anyone had done it since 1967. He was in the middle of three straight batting championships. Miggy was the American League MVP in 2012. He'd win it again in 2013. He and Justin Verlander were the best of a very good group of players. Every day of the season was exciting.

I'll always love this era of Tigers baseball.

I also love the '47 Brand Clean Up caps. For the longest time, I didn't care for unstructured hats. They just sat flat on top of my head, not looking or feeling that great. The '47 brand hats turned me around. They hug your head, providing a surprising amount of shape. I love the curved brim, too. The hats look great and feel old school. '47 Brand is my second-favorite hat after New Era.

Michigan Wolverines
Style: structured, fitted
By Nike
Bought at the Big House in Ann Arbor

Did I mention that my family loves football? We love it so much that, one year for Christmas, Jim bought us all a book about how to watch football better. It was fantastic.

In November 2012, we traveled to Michigan to see the Wolverines play the Iowa Hawkeyes on Saturday, then see the Lions host the Packers the next day. We had a bigger crew than our previous trip. Nancy, Shane, Curtis, and I were in for the adventure along with my parents, my brothers Jim and Scott, Scott's wife Natasha, and their five-month-old twins, Isaac and Savanne.

Scott's high school friend Brian Shannon lived in Ann Arbor and invited us to a tailgate party at the golf course across from the field before the game.

I had been to tailgate parties in Buffalo, but the tailgate party before the Michigan game was on another level.

Long tables, covered with canopies, contained dishes with a huge variety of breakfast foods. Pitchers of mimosas were plentiful. We weren't in a position to contribute food, but no one would let us pay, either. The Michigan pregame show was playing on a big screen, hooked up to a satellite dish, powered by a generator.

Nancy looked at me incredulously. "I think I have culture shock," she said. "This is where I see the difference between Americans and Canadians."

We'd been to a lot of games, but hadn't been hooked up like this, ever.

The game itself was everything we hoped it would be: 107,000 people, roughly the population of Thunder Bay, were packed into a bowl. We sat in the back of the endzone. The energy was high, and the band was playing. Curtis, just four, waved maize and blue pom poms and clapped his hands.

We sang the Michigan fight song, "Hail to the Victors," one of the first songs I learned all the words to. As we belted out "Hail, hail to Michigan, the leaders and the best," Shane made a face. "What about Ontario?" he asked. Shane thought about it for a second then announced, "I don't like this song."

What? How could a Colby not like "Hail to the Victors"?

I tried to explain the concept of a fight song. You're not going to get 100,000 people riled up with reasonable lyrics like: "We're pretty good and the other team is, too. Sometimes, they might be better than us."

It was futile. Shane wasn't down with that braggy tune.

Michigan won, so we left happy. I wore this excellent Michigan hat, the kind the coaches sport. I've always loved the colors and the block M, so I'm happy to have this cap.

The next day, we piled into Ford Field to see the Lions play the Packers. I wore my Billy Sims home jersey. Back in 1984—the last Lions game our full family had been to—they were destroyed by the Broncos. This year's Lions team was competitive though. Matthew Stafford was coming into his prime as a quarterback and Calvin Johnson was the dominant receiver in the league.

The boys followed me into the gift shop. I didn't want to get them anything too cool because I couldn't risk them bonding too strongly with the Lions. We know how that story ends. But we walked by a reasonably priced jersey and helmet combo.

Shane and Curtis looked up at me with their big blue eyes. When we took our seats, the boys each had a new helmet and jersey. Scott looked at me and said, "Helmets? Do you want them to become Lions fans?"

Scott was right to scold me. Curtis also had his face painted in silver and Honolulu blue. He looked like a little Lion. Curtis was so adorable he got on the Jumbotron. My kids have spent a lot of time on stadium screens.

We had a great time. My mom held little Isaac and Savanne in her lap while wearing the jersey of the dirtiest player in the league—Lions nose tackle Ndamukong Suh.

The game was close. The Lions trailed 21-20 with less than two minutes to play. Then the Lions threw four straight incomplete passes. We could see the coaches arguing on the sidelines. It was later revealed that Lions receiver Titus Young was intentionally sabotaging plays by lining up in the wrong spot. The Lions got the ball one more time, but Young wasn't on the field for that series. Detroit lost 24-20. Young was cut a few weeks later.

This is the kind of thing that happens to the Detroit Lions.

As a footnote, my kids liked the helmets but didn't become Lions fans. Crisis averted.

Pittsburgh Steelers
Style: unstructured, strapback
Made by '47 Brand

The Steelers were entirely worthy of becoming my sons' favorite team. I dressed both boys in Steelers gear since they were babies, but nothing solidifies a bond with a team like seeing them in person. In the fall of 2013, we traveled to Pittsburgh to reinforce their indoctrination. One November Saturday, Nancy and I packed Shane and Curtis—who were now nine and five, respectively—into our van and made the six-hour trip to Pittsburgh to see the Steelers play the Bills. We'd return on Sunday after the game.

The trip wasn't just for them, of course. I had only been to one Steelers home game and was anxious to get back to Heinz Field. The biggest drawback of being a fan of a team that plays in a different city is not being enveloped in that fandom. It's more than just being at the game. It's about being among your people. I wanted my kids to get a taste of Steeler Nation, but I was overdue for a big helping myself.

The game was on November 10, so it was a little chilly. No bother. We bundled up. Nancy brought a fleece Bills blanket because she likes to represent. We all had jerseys over our winter coats. I went with a Troy Polamalu home jersey I bought from Curtis's kindergarten teacher.

Our seats were in the front of the 200 level in the end zone. We had a great view. Early in the second quarter, Curtis, five, looked up at me and said, "Is the game almost over yet?"

"Not even close, buddy."

Curtis shut his eyes and fell asleep in my lap. He woke up in the fourth quarter. This was an expensive nap.

The game was fantastic, at least for me. The Steelers dominated, leading 23-3 late in the game. Nancy grumbled, "I wish the Bills would score at least one touchdown to make the trip worthwhile."

The Bills scored with five seconds left. There you go, baby. The Steelers won 23-10.

So, did this trip help indoctrinate my boys into Steeler fandom? Not really. They don't watch football, just the Super Bowl, but their rooting interest, when they have one, is with the Steelers. I keep hoping they'll come around to the sport someday.

As for the hat, once I fell for the '47 Brand, I started buying one for all of my favorite teams. I had to have one for the Steelers. Not only do the hats fit like a dream, but they're also elegantly simple—just a curved brim, the team colors and the logo in puff stitching. Perfection.

Detroit Tigers—Home
Style: structured, fitted
Made by New Era, 5950
Given to me at Detroit Tigers Fantasy Camp in 2014

This is my favorite hat because it's from the Detroit Tigers Fantasy Camp.

The camp was started by a salesman named Jerry Lewis in 1984. Hardcore Tigers fans paid for the chance to play games at the Tigers spring training facility in Lakeland, Florida, where they're coached by and mingle with former Tigers greats. At the end of the week, campers play the former Tigers. I had wanted to go since I first heard of it.

In 2014, the camp was celebrating the thirtieth anniversary of the Detroit Tigers last World Series Championship. My friend Larry suggested we go to celebrate our own milestones. I had turned fifty the previous July; he was turning fifty shortly after the camp. I desperately wanted to go, but it wasn't cheap.

I pitched the idea to Nancy, along with a financing plan. She said yes right away. Nancy knew what it meant to me. I immediately called Larry and said, "I'm in!"

In January 2014, we drove to Detroit and took batting practice at a cage inside Comerica Park. We met Jerry Lewis and some of the other campers. It was a chance to take some hacks and hang around in the visitors' locker room. That night, Larry and I saw the Red Wings beat the Los Angeles Kings.

The next day, we flew out of Detroit to Lakeland, home of the Tigers' spring training facility. Red Wings' retired star defenseman Chris Chelios was in line for security behind us. I told him, "You shouldn't have to show ID in this town. Just point to your face." My bon mot was not a conversation starter.

On the plane we saw some of the retired Tigers, including 1984 star pitcher Dan Petry. As we disembarked, I said hi to him.

"Have a good time," he said. "But remember Gates Brown's advice. Start slow and taper off. A lot of guys get injured."

We hopped on the bus from the airport to the training camp facility. 1984 Tigers starting pitcher Juan Berenguer, utility player Barbaro Garbey, and Ike Blessitt, a Tiger from the early 1970s, sat with us. The stories flowed, especially from an ebullient Berenguer. He told us how Yankees Hall-of-Famer Dave Winfield once charged the mound and knocked out Tigers starter Dave Rozema with one punch.

The 1984 Tigers World Champions were represented by Petry, Berenguer, Garbey, Rozema, Dave Bergman, Darrell Evans, Bill Fahey, John Grubb, Doug Bair, and Lou Whitaker. Sweet Lou would come later in the week but not as a coach.

The 1968 World Champion Tigers were represented by World Series MVP Mickey Lolich, Willie Horton, Jim Price, Jon Warden, and Canadian John Hiller, who arrived for the game against the campers.

The 1987 American League East Championship team was represented by Frank Tanana, Mike Heath, and Walt Terrell. Jake Wood, the first Black player drafted and developed by the Tigers came later in the week. Jack Billingham, who pitched a bit for the Tigers, but was better known as a starter on Cincinnati's Big Red Machine, was there early in the week.

The first day—when I walked into the clubhouse the Tigers use in spring training—I saw a Detroit Tigers' home jersey with my name and number hanging in a locker. I stopped and stared. "Colby 50" in midnight blue popped off a crisp white jersey. It was electric, surreal, and wonderful.

Larry and I were put on a team coached by Jon Warden and Willie Horton. They were a good combination. Warden pitched just one year in the majors, but it was with a World Championship team. He was big and gregarious. Warden was also the kangaroo court judge, fining people for uniform infractions and silly mistakes.

Willie Horton is a Tigers Legend. There is a statue of him at the stadium. Horton didn't learn our names but was super nice and told amazing stories all the time. He was still spry, despite using a walker. Horton used it to fend off two hard foul balls Larry hit right at him in the same at-bat.

Our team was fantastic. Two teammates who had been to about ten camps each said it was the most fun Fantasy Camp team they had ever been on. That had a lot to do with the Monash family. Three brothers, I'm guessing in their sixties or seventies, came with their three sons, ranging from early twenties to late thirties. They had talked about going for years, but when the eldest brother, Richard, had a cancer scare, they decided not to wait. The Monashes were doctors, lawyers, and teachers, except for the youngest, Zach, who was in his early twenties. Late in camp, Zach got a phone call telling him he'd been hired as a video researcher for the Kansas City Royals. The Monashes were salt of the Earth people—kind and fun.

When Lou Whitaker was looking for a place to sit at one of the evening events, Jon Warden placed him with the Monashes. I think Warden did that for Whitaker's benefit. Sweet Lou, who had been aloof, brightened in their company.

The big draw for the camp was hanging around with the former Major Leaguers. Walt Terrell bought me a beer, Darrell Evans was a trickster, Frank Tanana was loud and fun, Mike Heath talked about players he hated, and Lou Whitaker boogied near the stage while Larry and I sang "Detroit Rock City" on karaoke night. Dave Rozema knew the names of all the waitresses at Hooters. It was a blast.

The campers were just as fun. By the end of the week, everyone, players and campers, blended together. It's the dream of the hardcore sports fan to get to know the players as people. Juan Berenguer told me he went hunting and fishing with the campers. The line between fan and player was getting blurry.

All week, I posted pictures and game recaps on Facebook for my family and baseball fan friends to follow. It turned out to be a great document of the trip. I played fairly well, and, unlike most of my teammates, didn't spend any time in the trainers' room. Our team was competitive. We lost in the semi-finals on a huge blast in the last inning.

On the last day, we played the Tigers at Joker Marchant Stadium, the spring training home of the Tigers. I'd watched games from there for decades. Each team played two innings against the Tigers, so every player fielded once and got one at-bat. Coach Warden brought Larry and me out to sing the Canadian national anthem.

Before my at-bat, Jim Price, now an announcer for the Tigers, called out over the stadium loudspeaker, "Now coming to the plate, number fifty, Craig Colby." I stepped into the batter's box against Frank Tanana, with Mike Heath catching. They were the pitcher and catcher on the last day of the 1987 season when Tanana pitched a complete game, 1-0 victory to clinch the division. I watched that game from the centerfield bleachers at Tiger Stadium. They had both signed my scorecard from that game earlier in the week.

Camp veterans told me that this final game is great for the campers but is tough on the players, who basically play eighteen innings in their advanced years. I wasn't going to waste anyone's time. Tanana's first pitch was flat and in the middle of the plate. He'd served it up for me perfectly.

I swung and hit a hard one-hopper to Darrell Evans playing third. I took off, as well as my aching knees would let me after a week of playing two games a day. My foot hit first base just ahead of the throw to Dan Petry. Petry said, "Way to get down the line." Praise from a 1984 Tiger! Music to my ears. I later scored.

After the game, I didn't want the experience to end. I stayed in my uniform as long as possible. In the locker room, a group of enthralled campers listened to Willie Horton tell stories. Eventually, I took off my Tigers road uniform and headed to the shower. It was a big open room with shower heads in the outside wall. I washed the sweat out of my hair as warm water cascaded over me. I heard a voice a few feet away say, "The water pressure in here isn't very good, is it?"

I wiped the soap out of my eyes and looked over. It was Frank Tanana. I was in the shower room with one of my favorite Tigers pitchers ever. The line between fan and player evaporated.

After the camp was over, the Tigers delivered one more golden experience. In September, the campers went to Comerica Park in our personalized jerseys. My mom and dad came with me. I took them to our seats in the upper deck, then lined up with my Fantasy Camp friends out in centerfield. We descended into the concourse below Comerica Park, then emerged onto the grass in rightfield. As we walked out, I looked up at my folks and waved. They waved back.

My parents heard my name announced on the Comerica Park loudspeaker and saw my face on the big screen in leftfield. My parents have always been my biggest fans. There's no one I wanted there more. I felt like a kid again. Magic.

Atacama Large Millimeter Array

Style: unstructured
Given to me by Dan Hughes

In 2014 Blue Ant's nature channel Oasis was rebranded Love Nature and turned into an international streaming service in partnership with Smithsonian Channel in the US. My situation at Blue Ant had improved since the merger. I was named executive producer in charge of all our content, including an in-house production team.

We were now shooting everything in Ultra HD, basically 4K, which has four times the resolution of HD. Since that technology was emerging at the same time as affordable drones, we created a series featuring drones mounted with UHD cameras flying over some of the most beautiful landscapes in the world. Dan Hughes, an intelligent, soft-spoken guy with a gentle wit, produced that show. One of our locations was Chile. Not only is it spectacular, it's also high and dry, perfect for looking at objects in space. That's why the space observatory, the Atacama Large Millimeter Array, was built there. Dan brought me this hat because he knew I'd produced a lot of astronomy programs and love the subject. This hat is lightweight and provides a lot of shade, perfect for camping and outdoors stuff. It's special because Dan gave it to me.

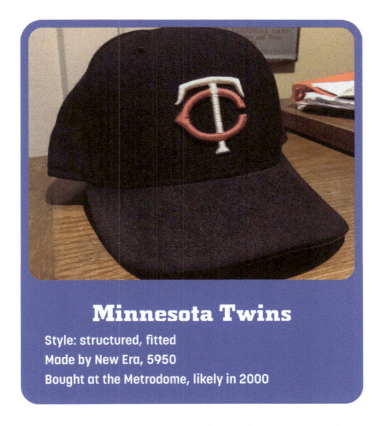

Minnesota Twins

Style: structured, fitted
Made by New Era, 5950
Bought at the Metrodome, likely in 2000

Minnesota was a frequent stop on the road trips Dave and I organized. We liked to leave from Thunder Bay early on a Thursday morning so we could pull into the Twin Cities in time for an afternoon getaway game, then we'd drive as far as we could towards our ultimate destination.

We were at the Metrodome in 1982 when the Minnesota Vikings beat the Dallas Cowboys despite Tony Dorsett's NFL record ninety-nine-yard run. I watched the last half of the play on my side in the aisle. Dave, a huge Cowboys fan, had knocked me over when he jumped up to cheer.

Snow was piled on the sidelines because the Metrodome's inflatable roof had collapsed the week before. It was the worst stadium ever, especially for baseball. It was like watching a game in a Tupperware container. A huge plastic drape hung on the rightfield wall. The roof was a gigantic white sheet.

The Metrodome had all the authenticity of Pat Boone singing Fats Domino songs. Olympic Stadium in Montreal was weird too, but at least it was weird and quirky, like Ally Sheady in "The Breakfast Club." The Metrodome was weird and offensive, like Judd Nelson in "The Breakfast Club."

When Target Field opened in 2010, I couldn't wait to see it. My Thunder Bay friends understandably lost interest in baseball trips when Dave died, so In July 2014, I went with my parents and my sons. It gave Nancy time with her family.

I don't think there's a team in sports that had a bigger upgrade than the Twins. Target Field is magnificent. It's a gorgeous open-air stadium with a tan limestone exterior. Statues of Twins greats stand guard outside, giving the new stadium a sense of history. Two separate outfield grandstands give the stadium a little height and majesty. The entrance to the outfield comes right off the street into a wide-open plaza. If you like visiting stadiums, this place is a must.

The Twins deserved a nice home. This franchise is the smart, hard-working kid in your class that stayed in her hometown, even though she could have been successful in the big city. If you saw a picture of the Twins on Facebook on vacation in Mexico looking fit, you wouldn't be jealous. You'd be happy for her. Despite playing in a small market, the Twins had drafted well-developed talent, were often competitive and even won a few championships but had to make do with an ugly house for a long time. They'd earned these fancy digs.

We saw a night game with my high school classmate Mark Moland, who had moved to Minneapolis, and his wife and daughters, and our family friends Andy and Larry Wamstad, who brought their kids, too. We had a great time in the rightfield stands, catching up and watching the game.

The next day, just the Colby clan watched a game from the upper deck behind home plate. Sharing this experience with my parents and Shane and Curtis was wonderful. Once I had kids, I looked at my mom and dad differently. I didn't appreciate everything my parents did for me until I started changing diapers, driving kids to hockey, and making my life subservient to my sons'. As your kids get older, you see them develop relationships with your parents. Age and youth have a lot in common. Both have more time to just be—explore their interests, enjoy the world. Those interactions exist outside of you, the middleman fully engaged juggling work, and bills, and marriage. You're often left out. A few hours in a gorgeous ballpark—letting go of the world and taking in the presence of your parents and children—is precious time.

By the way, I LOOOOOVE these Twins hats. The TC stands for the Twin Cities of Minneapolis and St. Paul (where I was born). The overlapping red and white TC on a midnight blue canvas is simple and classic. Everything about this hat is perfect.

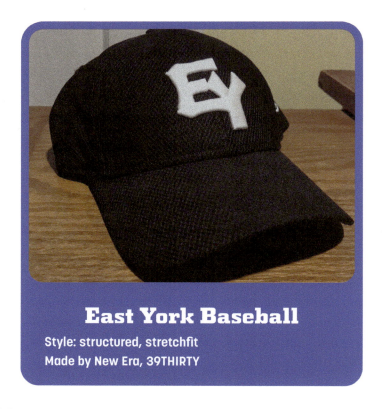

East York Baseball
Style: structured, stretchfit
Made by New Era, 39THIRTY

In 2015, the East York Baseball Association asked me to become a convener for one of their house league divisions. It looked like thankless work—forming teams, finding coaches, fielding complaints from parents—nothing that gives you the gratification of coaching kids. Still, I could see the value in it.

When I turned fifty, I became more aware of time. It's the real estate in our lives, valuable because it is limited. I'm not just talking about the time left in your life, but also the time in your day. I decided that creating an atmosphere where kids can enjoy sports was an excellent use of my time, so I signed on as the convener of Shane's division.

I continued to coach as well because that's the fun stuff. In our preseason meeting with the coaches, I set out my expectations. Our goals were to teach kids how to play and let them have fun. Nobody should be coaching like it's the majors. Kids would play every position and move throughout the batting order. The guidelines were already in place, but I wanted everyone to know that we would be playing by them.

When the season started, I said the same thing to the players and parents. The games are for the kids. A few more people stepped up to coach. Throughout the season, the other coaches and I discussed topics like how to handle pitching, and how to avoid losing streaks. I loved the job. I was also surprised to find out it wasn't thankless. The players' parents thanked me all the time.

The best part of it was looking out across the seven fields at Stan Wadlow Park, the home of the East York Baseball Association, and seeing the kids playing, and the families coaching and cheering. This was time perfectly spent.

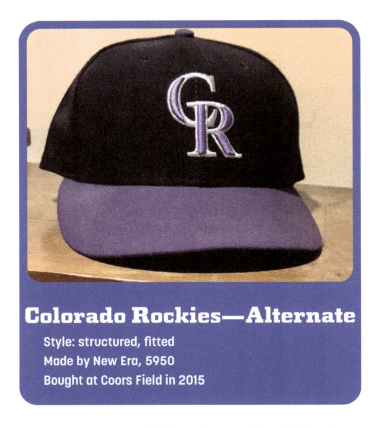

Colorado Rockies—Alternate
Style: structured, fitted
Made by New Era, 5950
Bought at Coors Field in 2015

In the fall of 2015, I attended the Jackson Hole Wildlife Film Festival in Jackson Hole, Wyoming. But first, I arranged a stopover in Denver for three reasons. The first was to visit my nephew Mitch, whom I hadn't seen in a long time. The second was to catch up with my Fantasy Camp buddy Chuck Steele. The third was to see a Colorado Rockies game at Coors Field.

I met my nephew at a restaurant near the stadium. Mitch, an outdoorsman who loves rock climbing, was fit and happy, with long hair and a big smile. Chuck Steele joined us after a while. Chuck Steele lives up to his name. He's a former University of California offensive lineman who crossed the NFL picket line to play for the Lions. Do you know how tough you have to be to cross the NFL picket line? Chuck Steele teaches military history to the military. Chuck Steele is not in the military. They need him more than he needs them. His Facebook cover picture is a photograph of sharks underwater. Chuck Steele took the picture himself. The sharks wisely kept their distance. As soon as Chuck Steele sat down, he started talking about religion and politics. He can do that. He's Chuck Steele.

We had seats in the lower deck near first base, about midway up. The skies were blue, and you could see the Rocky Mountains in the distance. The park is 100 percent charming, intimate, brick and steel. The bullpen is the best I've ever seen, beautifully landscaped. Big rocks and trees make the space look like a park. I'm surprised relievers don't refuse to come into the game. It's just too pretty out there to ever want to leave.

Because of the thin air in Denver, the Rockies seem to stock up on sluggers. They're like a tournament softball team. They show up in nice uniforms and beat the hell out of the ball. If they can't pitch all that well, who cares? The Rockies exist to outscore you.

The Rockies blew out the Los Angeles Dodgers, 12-5. Colorado third baseman Nolan Arenado went 2-3 with a home run and five RBIs. We had a great time. I bought a camo Rockies hat for Mitch and this one for me. I opted for a purple brim alternate hat because it gives the cap some flair. The silver stitching that frames the purple CR is a nice touch too. Great hat.

After the game Chuck went home and Mitch and I went to a restaurant to watch the Denver Broncos beat the Detroit Lions 24-12. The Broncos moved to 3-0, the Lions dropped to 0-3. Mitch is a Lions fan. We couldn't save him. I blame his dad, Jim.

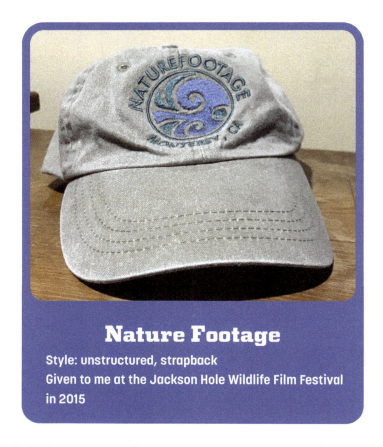

Nature Footage
Style: unstructured, strapback
Given to me at the Jackson Hole Wildlife Film Festival in 2015

One of the best parts of being a television executive is the conferences. Each one has its own flavor and they're often held in exciting locations. The World Congress of Science and Factual Producers is hosted by different cities each year. Thanks to that event, I've been to Manchester, England; Florence, Italy; Dresden, Germany; Paris, France; and Montreal, Canada.

The conference arranges trips to landmarks in each city. In Florence we toured the secret passages used by the Medici family, who were a political dynasty in the fifteenth century. The walls were lined with art. In Dresden we visited a church that had been bombed in World War II and was rebuilt fifty years later, after the Berlin wall came down. An organ player treated us to a recital that shook the building. Another conference, Sunnyside of the Doc, is in New Rochelle, France, on the coast. The Banff World Media Festival is held in the Canadian Rockies. At each of them, you learn about what's going on in the industry and make friends from around the world.

The Jackson Hole Wildlife Film Festival, now called Jackson Wild, is held at the Jackson Lake Lodge, with a spectacular view of the Teton Range section of the Rockies. From the back porch we could see a grizzly bear feeding on a moose carcass. At every break, I checked on that bear. My room was a nearby cabin. When I dropped off my bags, a fox brushed past my leg. A place that stunning can be a distraction. You want to skip your meetings and go for a walk. Some sessions though, you just can't miss. EO Wilson was the keynote speaker. He's perhaps the greatest living scientist, sometimes called Darwin's natural heir. Wilson told us that half the Earth should be protected space if we are to survive and live with nature. He's got that right.

I was given this hat by the owners of Nature Footage, a stock footage company specializing in the natural world, with whom we did a lot of work. It's super comfortable and I like the logo. Giveaway hats tend to be cheap, but this one is really nice. Thanks Nature Footage!

Detroit Tigers—Youper
Style: structured, snapback
Giveaway at Comerica Park in 2016

Nancy stopped joining us on baseball trips to Detroit. She didn't like sitting in a car for four hours to sit in a stadium, to sit in a car on the way back. That's fine. Some boys' time was welcome all the way around.

I started booking trips on Mother's Day Weekend in May. I'd take the kids out of school early on Friday, we'd drive down for the night game, stay in a hotel, go to the game on Saturday then drive home. We'd be back in Toronto for Mother's Day on Sunday. Part of her present was our absence. Sometimes we'd go to the game with family in Michigan, like my Aunt Donna, Uncle Tom and their daughter, my cousin Robyn. Sometimes we'd go with Fantasy Camp friends. Sometimes it would be just us.

The boys and I developed some nice traditions, the biggest of which was a game called "Don't Scare the Horsey." It took place in the unsupervised hotel pool. I was the horsey. One of the boys would hop on my back, then I'd walk around the pool and say, "Don't scare the horsey." The other boy would wait for the right moment, then say, "boo," startling the horsey. I would jump around, trying to buck the rider off my back. "Don't Scare the Horsey" was a staple of every baseball trip and day at the beach.

At the game, Shane would always try to start the wave. He was super cute. On one trip, strangers admired his persistence and exuberance so much, they bought him cotton candy. Another time, he got a wave to go all the way around the stadium while I was buying pizza for us.

Curtis decided he would be a Tigers fan, so I wouldn't have to cheer for them by myself. I told him he could cheer for whomever he wanted, but he was committed to his choice.

On the 2016 trip, we were given these Youper hats. Youper is what people in Michigan call residents of the Upper Peninsula, the part of the state that doesn't look like a mitten. Hunting and fishing are popular up there. Curtis loved the hat so much it became his go-to Tigers cap.

We also were shown on the Jumbotron during the Lion King gimmick. You hold your child over your head, like Rafiki did to Simba in the movie. I held up Curtis, now eight, far larger than the other children who made it on camera. Shane was beside us, ceremoniously holding up a bag of popcorn.

I love, love, love those trips with my boys.

Baltimore Orioles—Alternate

Style: structured, fitted
Made by New Era, 5950
Bought in the late-2000s.

Darcy and Sue Hagberg responded to their son Dave's death differently. Sue would go for long walks alone. I knew this is when she would process her pain, alone, away from prying eyes. Darcy said Sue was put on Earth to take care of children, a role she embraced. There was no way she'd put herself in a position to be taken care of.

When I'd come home to Thunder Bay, I'd drop by their house on Elm Street and sit on a stool in the kitchen. Sue would talk about people who approached her in the street to tell her Dave was not himself in that terrible moment. They knew because at one point they had been in the same dark place.

Some had woken up in the hospital and didn't believe it when they were told of their attempt. Others would tell her they remembered everything, but it was like someone else was doing it. They all told Sue that Dave was under an influence outside his personality.

Sue would tell me, "What can you do? We're all OK."

It only took one look at Darcy, arms crossed, head down, wandering around the room, to know that wasn't true.

Darcy's gruffness was a paper-thin veil over his reflective soul. He talked about real things. Darcy wasn't afraid to be part of humanity's vulnerable heartbeat. He was not OK after Dave died, but Darcy stood in that fire, even while it burned him.

In 2015, I found out that Sue had cancer. When she came to Toronto for surgery, I booked the day off work. That morning, while it was still dark, I drove to the hotel where she was staying with Darcy, their daughter Val, Val's daughter Amy, and Sue's sister Colleen. I picked them up for the drive to the hospital. We'd only been in the car for three minutes before everybody started criticizing the dirtiness of my windshield.

I replied, "That took longer than I thought it would."

I sat with my second family, each of us hoping for news contrary to our expectations. It was both horrible and wonderful. How much time do you have with the people you love? When you know it is running out, even sitting in uncomfortable chairs in a hospital waiting room is a moment cherished beyond gold.

In the spring of 2017, we knew the end was near. I flew home to Thunder Bay to see Sue one last time. She was bedridden, so visits to her were like being granted an audience. You'd walk in the room, and there she was, in her bed, waiting to receive you with a commanding dignity.

We talked. I took her lead, keeping it light or diving deep, depending on her mood. When she wanted to go into the living room, someone would carry her. A couple of times that someone was me, and the moment revealed her most defining characteristics. She bristled in pain when I lifted her. Then she said "It's OK, Craig. You're doing good." Sue's fleecy kindness often obscured her iron will.

Before I left Thunder Bay, knowing we would never see each other again, Sue told me what I'm sure she told everyone.

"If I die tomorrow, be happy for me," she said. "I'm going to see my son, my sister, and my mother."

On Monday, April 3, 2017, we lost Sue Hagberg. I was happy for her. We all knew what she really wanted was to be with Dave. But I was sad for the rest of us.

I hold onto things that help me feel close to the Hagbergs. Because Dave was an Orioles fan, this hat is one of them. I bought this Orioles hat at a sale at the Blue Jays gift shop. The colors and simple style of this hat look great. I also like that it's a nod to the nickname for the team's nickname; the Orioles are often referred to as the Os. That makes this hat feel friendly and familiar.

Thunder Bay Whiskey Jacks
Style: structured, fitted
Made by New Era, 5950

A Thunder Bay resident named Greg Balec was working for the Thunder Bay Border Cats when he noticed how often people wore Whiskey Jacks gear. So, he called the former owner of the Whiskey Jacks, Rickey May, and bought the rights to the logo. Then Greg made hats and sold them online. Guess what? He made money!

I always regretted not buying a proper, fitted Whiskey Jacks road cap, so I ordered one on eBay right away. I realized later that the TB needed to be teal, not purple, to be historically accurate. Still, this is a badass hat. I later bought the hat below, with a teal TB and brim, a style the team wore in their final season, 1998. Man, I love the Whiskey Jacks gear. Not only do they have great colors and classic logo, but they bring me back to a happy time in my life when I was falling in love with Nancy. The Jacks hat still look great and so does my wife.

I also found a Whiskey Jacks home jersey on eBay. It was white with teal pinstripes with "Jacks" written across the front in purple. Apparently, someone had bought a box of unused gear when the team went under, and this jersey was from that lot. I bought it right away. I'm glad I ordered it when I did, because by the time it arrived my life had changed dramatically.

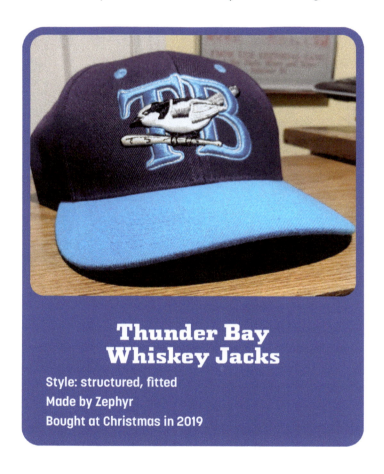

Thunder Bay Whiskey Jacks
Style: structured, fitted
Made by Zephyr
Bought at Christmas in 2019

Toronto Blue Jays
Style: structured, fitted
Made by New Era, 5950

In late April 2017, I was called to a meeting at work with the head of my department, Vanessa Case. When I noticed it would be just the two of us, I knew something was up. I was steeled for bad news when I walked into her office and closed the door behind me. Vanessa got right to the point. Changes were being made to Love Nature and I wouldn't be part of them. My job was moving to Washington, DC, and I wasn't going with it. She said my work was good and all I had done for the company was appreciated. We had a nice discussion. I had been hoping for a package for a few years and their offer was fair. Blue Ant handled a difficult situation with kindness and class.

The next day, I was allowed to address my team. I had some time to kill beforehand, so I dropped in on my friend Bob Paajanen, who lived close to the office. I told him my news. Then he told me his. Bob was losing his job, too. We sat on his front porch, discussing our uncertain futures. Then, I went in for the meeting announcing my departure and that others would be losing their jobs, as well.

Coincidentally, I had plans to go to the Blue Jays game the next weekend with my family, Bob's family, Scott's family, our friend Laura Boast, and my niece Danielle. Bob and I were trying to stay positive, but we were two men in our mid-fifties, both fathers to children aged thirteen and nine. Instead of cruising into retirement, we were becoming less employable right when we needed to be able to provide for our children's education. We were both scared.

I wore this hat, a Jays' home 5950—royal blue with a sleek logo, one of the most beautiful hats in baseball—as the fourteen of us sat in the upper deck, doing our best to enjoy the game. When hard times come, we seek refuge in the familiar, and a baseball game certainly fit that bill for me. Even more, we need the company of family and true friends. It wasn't just that Bob and I were walking the same difficult road. We had known each other since we were teens.

There is a shorthand in those long-term friendships that forgoes the need for long explanations. You just know. We were lucky to have that, lucky to have smart wives with good jobs, and lucky to have a day like this already scheduled. We had support in person right when we needed it. After the game, we went back to Bob and Jen's for pizza, the kids playing video games while the adults talked, wrapping up a day that was both uneasy and comforting.

Detroit Tigers—Road
Style: structured, fitted
Made by New Era, 5950

I decided to form my own company, naming it colbyvision on the advice that if I was consulting or coaching, the company should include my name. After six weeks of networking, I was offered a great job producing a history series by one of my favorite people in the industry, Bree Tiffin. She was the associate producer on the first series I produced back in 1998. This time, she'd be the executive producer. I'd be reporting to her.

I loved working with Bree. She'd put together a great team, filled with many of the Love Nature crew. The job was rewarding and fun, with some good travel. I could enjoy the craft of television again. I was happy and relaxed.

When the Tigers came to Toronto later that year, Curtis and I went to one of the games. Shane had always been daddy's boy, and Curtis naturally gravitated to Nancy. As Curtis got older, he sought out ways for us to be close. I'm sure choosing to be a Tigers fan was one.

Curtis and I sat in the upper deck. I was wearing this hat and a Tigers jacket. Curtis wore his Youper hat and a Tigers lightweight jacket we'd bought at Comerica Park. This was a memorable game. The Tigers' Nick Castellanos hit a grand slam in the third inning. In the sixth inning, the Tigers' Jeimer Candelario picked up a hot grounder at third, touched the bag, fired to Ian Kinsler covering second who threw it to Efren Navarro at first. Triple play! This was just the seventh time in Major League Baseball history a team had hit a grand slam and turned a triple play in the same game. Shane Greene struck out the last batter to preserve a 5-4 Tigers win.

This was a great night at the park with Curtis, my son and fellow Tigers fan.

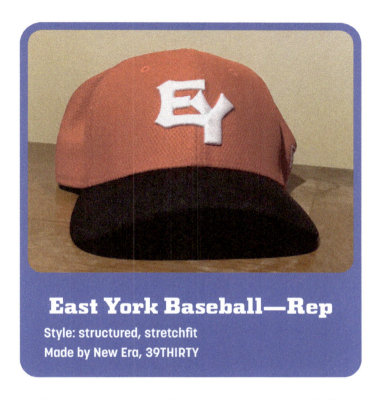

East York Baseball—Rep
Style: structured, stretchfit
Made by New Era, 39THIRTY

In 2018, I became a Vice President at the East York Baseball Association, in charge of the house league—with 750 kids and 1,500 parents. I stopped coaching to focus on working with the conveners and resolving any conflicts with players, parents, and coaches.

Most nights I'd spend time at Stan Wadlow Park, walking between the diamonds, talking to coaches and parents, watching kids have fun. I'd wear a black EY golf shirt with "executive" stitched on the sleeves, or an EY windbreaker or hoodie. The black EY house league hat was on my head most nights. I had nothing to do with rep baseball, the most competitive division, other than recruiting rep players and coaches to help on skill development days. I'm strictly a house league guy. I was never the best athlete, and my north star is providing a fun experience for players of all abilities. However, I loved the rep hats, so I bought one just to mix it up, since I was wearing an East York baseball hat four nights a week. Was I dressed in borrowed robes? Maybe, but it was a sweet-looking family robe.

Pittsburgh Steelers—
2007 Division Champions
Style: structured, Velcro strapback
Made by Reebok

Fellow Steelers fans Kevin Francisco and Seonaid Eggett picked up this hat for me at the Steelers training camp in Latrobe, Pennsylvania. Division Championship hats don't carry much sway, especially for a team that's won so many Super Bowls. Kevin and Seonaid know this. This hat probably didn't cost much either, for the same reason. They know I know that, too. What makes this hat so great though, is that my fellow Pittsburgh Steelers fans wanted to share their experience with me. I love that. The hat is a bit misshapen because I wore it a lot when I went running in the summer.

Kevin, Seonaid, and our fellow Steelers fan Forbes Robertson watch games together, but from our own individual homes. We have a running text chain where we comment on plays and share GIFS. Seonaid plans clever GIFs ahead of time to drop on us at key points in the game. Last season, she followed every touchdown with some crazy dance GIF. We let Larry join, too, even though he's not a Steelers fan.

Kevin and Forbes are also Montreal Canadiens fans. They started using the chat stream for Habs games. My phone kept pinging with Hab-fan banter, so I had to ask them to make a different chain. Friendship has its limits.

I text Scott and Jim during games, too, usually the nationally televised broadcasts on Sunday and Monday nights. For the fans, football is more than just watching the games. Interacting with other fans becomes part of the glue that holds relationships together. When Dave died in 2005, I created a couple of football pools to have frequent, fun contact with his wife and sons. My family joined, as well. In one pool, we pick a winner against a point spread, which gives the stronger team a handicap. The better team must win by a certain number of points. The other pool is a knockout format. You pick one team to win per week and can't pick the same team twice. Once you lose, you're out. The pools are essential to the season for us now. Jim, Scott, and I have each won both pools. Jim will spend time researching each team before making his picks and will talk to Dad on the phone several times a week just about the pool. My dad loves it. He's won the picks vs. the spread pool but skips the knockout pool.

Jim, Scott, and I lead busy lives. Jim is a vice-president and treasurer for Honeywell, a high-powered job that eats a lot of his time. You might think he was the most successful Colby. I think that title goes to Scott. He's a best-selling author and, far more importantly, in charge of the opinions page at the Toronto Star. Being paid to rule over opinions is the most Colby job in existence. Despite those obligations, we come together over football and the pools are instrumental.

Shane, Curtis and Nancy have joined the pool sporadically, with some good results. In 2009, Nancy tied my dad and my cousin Lou for most wins but lost the tiebreaker—guessing how many points would be scored in the Monday night game every week. Jim asked Nancy how she made her picks.

Nancy told him, "I alternate between Shane and Curtis weeks. During a Shane week, I pick the team whose name has the most letters in common with "Shane." In Curtis weeks, I pick the team whose name has the most letters in common with "Curtis."

When Jim heard that, I think a little part of him died.

In 2019, Shane won the knockout pool by picking the team favored by the most points every week. He didn't watch one game all year. In fact, my wife and kids only watch the Super Bowl. They enjoy going to games, and like wearing the gear, but it's just not their thing, despite the years I've spent trying to indoctrinate them.

That's OK. My kids don't have to find common ground with me. I have to find common ground with them. In English class, Shane was asked to bring an object from home and tell stories about it (a technique that should be familiar to readers of this book by now). He brought in video game controllers, then told his classmates about the great times he had playing Lego Batman and the Batman Arkham games with me.

Shane and Curtis play hockey and I've coached on both of their house league teams, despite never playing the game myself. I listen to what the other coaches say then shout it at the players on the ice during the game, hopefully at the right moments. As a family, we go to Marvel movies and watch the shows on television together. My boys are Marvel kids, just like I was, and Nancy enjoys those stories, too. Our common ground is different than the one I enjoy with my parents and brothers.

My job as a dad isn't to get them to love football like I do. It's to make sure they know that they are loved and supported unconditionally, no matter what life throws at them. I do my best to be up to that task every single day.

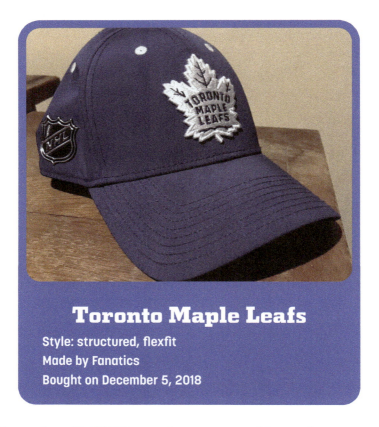

Toronto Maple Leafs
Style: structured, flexfit
Made by Fanatics
Bought on December 5, 2018

On December 3, 2018, my fourteen-year-old son Shane was in the hospital. He'd been running a fever, with a bad headache and a runny nose for a little more than a week. We'd been to the doctor twice before we took him into emergency the day before. Since then, he'd become delirious. About twelve hours after he was admitted, he couldn't remember his brother Curtis's name. This shook my wife Nancy, who had been with him overnight. The doctor said Shane probably had viral meningitis, which would have to run its course. Shane was on painkillers and antibiotics.

At three o'clock that afternoon, I was writing a script, facing Shane's bed in case he needed anything. Shane moaned. I hurried over to him. "Do you want some water?" He nodded. I put the cup to his lips and poured some in his mouth. Shane gurgled.

"Shane, are you choking?" His answer was unintelligible. When Shane spoke, only the left side of his mouth moved. I looked into my son's eyes and saw him falling away from me. My beautiful boy was slipping into darkness, and I didn't know if he'd ever come back.

I opened the door and called for help. The nurse and doctor came in. They asked Shane who I was. He mumbled, "Uncle Scott." My son didn't recognize me. He didn't know I was there for him. The doctor said, "I think he's having a stroke." I called Nancy to tell her. Then I came apart.

You'd think the room would fill with surgeons and nurses making quick calls to the imaging department. None of that happened. The hospital we were in wasn't equipped to handle this situation, so they arranged a transfer to SickKids Hospital in downtown Toronto. While we waited, I was alone in the room with Shane, wondering if my quirky, joyful boy would ever emerge.

Nancy arrived at about 4:45 p.m., a pillar of calm and positive energy. I'd been crying since I called her. I felt like I'd been hollowed out.

At 5:15, the ambulance arrived. Nancy rode with Shane in case a decision needed to be made. I was in no shape to do that, so I drove our van to SickKids.

When I walked into their emergency room, the change in hospital was visceral. It felt like ocean air hitting my face. "Hello, I'm Dr. Ahmed. I'm a neurosurgeon." Calm, but acknowledging the gravity of the situation, they asked us questions. Another doctor said, "We're enacting stroke protocol. That will get us into an MRI right away."

Dr. Ahmed said that if it was a stroke, Shane needed to have medication within four hours or there could be permanent brain damage. It was after 6 p.m., and I'd noticed the change in Shane at 3 p.m. Were we already too late? Dr. Ahmed said, "If we give him the medication and we're wrong, the results will be devastating."

At 6:40 p.m., we were outside the MRI. The technician was asking Nancy to fill out a form so she could sit in the room with Shane while he was inside the machine. I looked at the technician and said as calmly as possible, "Can we hurry this up? Time is not on our side here." I turned to Dr. Ahmed and asked, "Right?" He nodded gravely.

Within five minutes, Shane was in the MRI. I went to waiting-room-purgatory where families watched me struggle to keep it together. I wasn't successful.

Shortly after 7 p.m., Nancy and Dr. Ahmed rushed out, and Dr. Ahmed delivered the news.

"Fluid from a sinus infection has leaked into his brain. We'll have surgery to remove it tonight."

I was relieved. At least we knew what it was and what could be done.

Another neurosurgeon joined us after Shane's bed was wheeled back to emergency. She said, "He's going to be fine. The recovery will be long, but he'll be fine. There's no probing into the brain. We just need to clean the fluid off the surface."

I held onto that statement like a drowning man clutches a life preserver.

Nancy and I had a decision to make. One of us had to stay for the surgery and the other had to go home to take care of Curtis, who had been picked up from school by our friend Melissa. Both of our children needed us. Since I still didn't trust myself to make a decision, we agreed that I'd go home, and Nancy would stay.

I relieved Melissa and told Curtis that Shane was having surgery. Curtis understood how serious this was, but he was calm and brave. I told him he could sleep in my bed with me that night. Once Curtis was asleep, I turned on the TV, sat on the couch with the phone and waited. Surgery started at 9 p.m. At about 11:30 p.m., Nancy called.

"They're really happy with the operation," she said. "Now the ear, nose, and throat surgeons have to fix his nasal cavity."

That would take another hour. Nancy called at 1 a.m. and told me the second surgery had been successful. I went to bed.

When I arrived at the hospital the next morning, Shane was in the intensive care unit with a tube down his throat and a green cap on his head with a note taped to it. NO BONE was written in large letters. Most of the left side of his skull had been removed to relieve the swelling and remove the fluid.

Shane couldn't talk or move his right side, but he could squeeze his left hand. I spent the day holding it. How much did he know? How much damage had been done? Was my son still in there?

Shane has always been reciprocal. If you put your arm around him, he'll put his arm around you. If you pat his back, he'll pat yours. I was moving my thumb over Shane's left hand. Shane responded, moving his finger across my hand. That's when I knew my son was still in there.

Nancy arrived to take the night shift. In the middle of the night, my phone beeped. It was a text from Nancy. The tube had been removed from Shane's mouth. He had started to talk a little and, most importantly, he had moved his right arm and leg a little. Incredible! The next morning, as I was getting ready to go into the hospital, I got another text from Nancy, "The Maple Leafs will be here today!"

I didn't care. Would Shane even know the players were there? Both boys were playing select hockey, Shane for the Leaside Hockey Association and Curtis for the East York Hockey Association, so they had jerseys with their names on the back. I told Nancy I'd bring the boys' jerseys. Maybe the Leafs could hold them up for a picture.

I arrived to find that Shane could speak a few words at a time. His eyes were almost swollen shut, and his head drooped to his right. He was in and out of consciousness. Alexis, who oversaw the Leafs' visit, came by. I gave her the boys' jerseys. She couldn't make any promises. I told her that it was OK. I knew she'd be busy all day and I just needed the jerseys back. I didn't give it another thought.

In the early afternoon, a nurse said, "The Leafs are coming to see Shane. They'll be here in five minutes."

I ran over to Shane and said, "The Maple Leafs are coming to see you."

"Oh gosh!" he said.

"Do you want that?"

"Yes!"

The nurse and I swung the bed around to face the door. Only two visitors at a time were allowed in an intensive care room, so the players wouldn't be able to come in.

As soon as the bed was in place, I looked down the hall. Frederik Andersen, Zach Hyman, Travis Dermott and Kasperi Kapanen, wearing the Leafs' blue jerseys, were walking our way.

The players looked into Shane's room. Shane jerked his head fully upright, pushed open his eyes and smiled. I didn't know he was capable of any of those things.

The Leafs said, "Hi."

Shane replied, "Hi."

The players told him to get better soon. Shane gave them a thumbs up. He used his right hand, which he couldn't move the previous day.

Alexis later told me in her seventeen years on the job, she had never seen a reaction like Shane's from a child so sick.

I quickly took pictures of the players with both the boys' jerseys, then shots with individual jerseys. I tried to thank the players. Nothing came out. I just stood there, tears streaming down my cheeks. Zach Hyman patted my arm. "Thank you," I finally croaked.

The Leafs gave me a gift bag for Shane and another one for Curtis. "Double your pleasure," Kapanen said as they left.

That was the moment I became a Toronto Maple Leafs fan.

On my way home that night, I bought this Toronto Maple Leafs hat. I wore it as I watched their next game. It was against the Red Wings, my favorite team for more than twenty-five years. I cheered for the Leafs without reservation.

Shane recovered remarkably quickly.

In just a few days, he was moved from the intensive care unit to a private room. The movement on the right side of his body returned quickly. Nancy and I had to help him start walking again, but he took to it well. Shane was impressively good-natured throughout the ordeal.

Shortly after the surgery, his friend Meredith Paajanen, Bob's daughter, visited Shane. She was understandably shaken by the sight of Shane's half shaven head and huge scar.

"Wow!" she said. "You just start high school and then you have brain surgery."

'Ah, it's not as bad as it seems," Shane said nonchalantly.

It was the coolest thing I've ever seen.

The real issue was the left side of his head where his skull was missing. There was no timetable for replacing it. Shane's brain was covered only by a membrane and a layer of skin. The left side of Shane's head was bald, because it was shaved for surgery, and bulging, because of the huge fluid buildup.

The skin dropped off the left side of his skull where the bone was removed, hanging like a blanket over a chair, then looked like a water balloon. Once the fluid dissipated, Shane would be fitted with a helmet to protect his brain. Then he could leave the hospital. As Christmas approached, the fluid was still prominent. We knew we'd be in SickKids over the holidays.

Nancy and I embraced it. We hung stockings and strung up lights in the hospital room. At least we'd be together. My parents, Scott, Natasha, and their twins Isaac and Savanne visited on December 22. Curtis wasn't talking to anyone. He sat with his head resting on a table.

Then my folks and Scott's family left for Jim's cottage in Muskoka, where they would spend Christmas. It was my turn to stay with Shane overnight. A bench with drawers underneath doubled as a bed when you covered it with linens and threw on a pillow. Nancy and I had been trading off every day. The hospital doesn't recommend caregivers staying for more than two nights in a row. When the caregivers get worn down, nurses need to deal with two patients.

The next day, I sent Nancy a text. "We're going to have Christmas at SickKids and it's going to be awesome. All that matters is that we're together. We're unstoppable!"

She replied, "Call me."

Curtis had a headache and a fever, the same symptoms Shane had before we brought him to the hospital. Nancy had to take Curtis to the doctor. Even if he was fine, Curtis had to be two days' fever free before he could come visit Shane. Since Nancy was caring for Curtis, and had been exposed, we couldn't switch spots.

Our family was going to be apart at Christmas. That was the least of our concerns though. Could Curtis have the same illness as Shane? We didn't take any chances. Curtis went back and forth to the walk-in clinic and the doctor's office. We were told that Curtis just had a seasonal flu. If the fever continued, he should see a doctor again.

On Christmas Day, Santa and Buddy the Elf visited Shane, and then Shane and I exchanged a few gifts. Because Curtis still had a fever, he and Nancy spent five hours in SickKids' emergency room. I put on a mask and went down to say hello. We had the best Christmas we could.

Still, we were in a tempest of uncertainty. How long would Curtis be ill? How long would Shane be in the hospital? When would his skull be repaired? We found a coping mechanism to deal with the unknowns. Since looking back was scary, and looking forward made us anxious, we stayed in the moment. Since Shane was doing well and was in an incredible hospital, the present was the safest place to be.

Shane and I developed a daily routine of walking, meals, medication, and showers. At night we'd watch the Maple Leafs or a movie that was too grown up for Curtis to see. Both of us enjoyed those nights together. A lot. We still talk about them fondly.

On January 1, we could finally be together, so we had our family Christmas. Shane had been campaigning for a PS4 ("I don't know, Shane. Do you think you've earned it?"). When Shane and Curtis pulled back the wrapping paper to reveal their heart's desire, both boys' faces exploded into smiles. We spent the rest of the day taking turns being Spider-Man in the latest game.

That night, I went home with Curtis. I also went home with a piece of chicken stuck in my throat from our Christmas dinner. I couldn't clear it for hours, so I called Telehealth, the province's medical guidance line. I asked if I had to go to emergency in the morning or if I could go to a walk-in clinic. "You have to be in a hospital in an hour!"

After midnight, I dropped Curtis off at Scott's all the way across town, then went to Toronto General Hospital, because it's across the street from SickKids, where I had paid for monthly parking. The next day I was rolled into an operating room where a surgeon hauled a chunk of chicken out of my throat.

And that's the kind of Christmas it was for the Colbys in 2018.

I wore this hat exclusively during my time in the hospital. It was perfect—light and flexible with a nicely structured front. I love this version of the Leafs' logo, with the ragged edges and lines. It feels classic. Also, wearing a hat for a new favorite team this late in my sports fandom reminded me that things were different now. Facing change wasn't enough. I needed to commit to it.

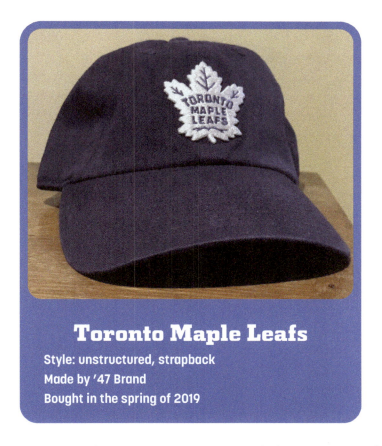

Toronto Maple Leafs
Style: unstructured, strapback
Made by '47 Brand
Bought in the spring of 2019

I can't overstate how strange it is to switch favorite teams. It's like altering your DNA. If that hospital visit had been our only encounter with the Leafs, it would have been enough to justify the change. However, the Leafs kept coming through for our family.

Shane was in the hospital for five weeks. Before we left, we were asked if Shane would like to go to a game and meet the coach, Mike Babcock. Of course! We decided Nancy would take Shane to the game. Then SickKids offered us two more tickets, so our whole family could attend.

When game night arrived, Shane had moved from SickKids to Holland Bloorview Children's Rehabilitation Hospital. I picked up Curtis after school, then Shane. Between the time we left Holland Bloorview and the time we arrived at the parking lot near the arena, Shane had thrown up a few times. This wasn't unusual. He sometimes reacted to the medication, so I kept plastic bags in the car just in case. We met Nancy at the gate and she and Curtis headed to their seats. Shane and I went to another entrance to meet the Maple Leafs' staff.

Shane sat back on a chair and closed his eyes. He looked pale. When the Leafs' staff arrived, I said, "I don't think we're going to make it." I asked Shane if he wanted to go back to the hospital. He said he wanted to meet the coach first.

We were led through the hallways to Babcock's office. After a few minutes, the door swung open, and Coach Babcock greeted us. He was friendly, giving Shane his full attention. I told him Shane wasn't feeling well and wouldn't be able to stay for the game. Babcock said, "Don't you worry about it. You can come back to another game. We'll bring you to a practice, too."

We left the office and went straight to a bathroom where Shane was sick several more times. Leafs staff brought a wheelchair and rolled Shane all the way back to the car.

Sure enough, Shane and I were invited back to another game and the whole family was invited to the morning practice. Christine Nicholson from the Leafs gave Shane a personalized Leafs jersey, with his name and number on the back. Before the game, we had another audience with Coach Babcock, who asked Shane about his interests and told him that his injury will make him more compassionate, and that compassion is the true measure of a man.

A few weeks later, when Shane was having a checkup at SickKids Hospital, he was invited to meet Leafs superstar Auston Matthews, who was visiting that day. Auston was gregarious, greeting a group of kids and parents. He made a batch of slime with the SickKids staff, then Matthews talked with the patients and their families.

Shane had a chance to ask a question of Toronto's greatest hockey player in a generation. Shane seized the moment. He asked Auston, "Is a hot dog a sandwich?" The Leafs superstar jumped at the question. Matthews insisted that it was not. He told us that, in Columbus, some fans held up a sign that said "Auston Matthews thinks a hot dog is a sandwich." Matthews hated that sign! "That's not what I think at all!" Then Matthews autographed Shane's jersey (not his personalized one) and posed for a few pictures.

Shane's illness was a rough stretch for our whole family. The Toronto Maple Leafs went out of their way to bring us a little happiness. We're fans for life.

Naturally, I had to get a '47 Brand unstructured Maple Leafs hat so I could throw a cap in a bag for road trips without worrying about it getting crushed. It bears repeating, the '47 hats are outstanding.

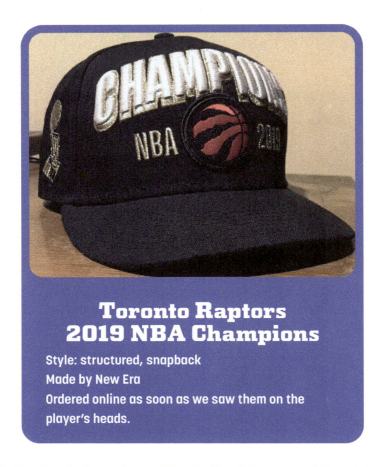

Toronto Raptors 2019 NBA Champions

Style: structured, snapback
Made by New Era
Ordered online as soon as we saw them on the player's heads.

Christine Nicholson from Maple Leaf Sports and Entertainment, who had been our point person on the Leafs tickets, texted me during the Raptors' playoff run in the spring of 2019. Did we want tickets to a Raptors' playoff game? Yes!

So, all four of us geared up and met her outside the stadium for Game Two of the conference semi-finals against the Philadelphia 76ers. We had seats along the baseline, halfway up the lower bowl. The combined face value of the tickets was more than $1,000. We cheered our lungs out for Kawhi Leonard, Kyle Lowry, and the Raptors. The Raps lost that game, unfortunately, but we were all in for the playoff run.

At night, Nancy and I took turns treating Shane's wound from his surgery. The incision started above his right eyebrow, went across the top of his head, then looped around the back of his head and ended above his left ear. We had to dab it with Vaseline every night. That's what we were doing when Kawhi Leonard hit his miracle, four-bounce-on-the-rim, series-clinching shot in Game Seven. We launched off the couch in euphoria. The first thing the next morning, we showed Curtis "The Shot."

After that, we watched every playoff game together. When the kids went to bed, we'd record the rest of the game so they could watch it in the morning.

Like the rest of Toronto—and Canada, for that matter—we were fully invested. For us however, the Raptors were a joyous lifeline while we endured Shane's illness.

The Raptors clinched the championship on June 13, 2019, Shane's fifteenth birthday. We hugged each other and cheered. I ordered these hats for myself and the boys as soon as we saw them on the players' heads. Nancy didn't want one. Then we ran out in the street and hugged the neighbors. John, a couple of doors down, had two Raptors flags in front of his house. He let Shane and Curtis carry them down the street as we waved to passing cars.

Even though my favorite teams had won some championships, I hadn't had this experience since the Tigers won the World Series in 1984. That's the downside of cheering for out-of-town teams. Being part of the citywide joy made this win extra-special. It felt great to be part of victory that enveloped the whole community.

A few days later, Shane, Curtis, Shane's buddy Ethan, and I went downtown for the parade. It was hot and crowded, and I worried about Shane in that environment with his hot black helmet. After two hours of being jostled by sweaty humanity without seeing the Raptors, Curtis leaned into me and said, "I can't do this anymore." We went to an air-conditioned restaurant to watch the festivities in comfort and eat some good food.

After the speeches were over, we walked up Yonge Street, past the corner of Queen Street, on our way back to the subway. We heard a loud "POP! POP! POP!"

Curtis asked, "What's that?"

"I don't know."

"Are those gunshots?"

"I don't know." But I did.

We flagged a cab and went home.

Once inside, we turned on the TV and heard that there were gunshots in Nathan Phillips Square, a few blocks from where we were walking. Four people were injured, none of them critically.

Later that afternoon, I asked the boys if they had a good time. They all said no. I asked them if they were happy that we went to the parade. They all said yes.

It was a bittersweet moment in a bittersweet year. One thing is certain, we loved this epic championship hat. It screams accomplishment! Curtis wore his every day. When Shane's head was repaired, and he could wear a hat again, this was the first one he put on. But we're getting ahead of ourselves on that point.

TSN—New Logo
Style: structured, strapback

The place where you started your career is always going to feel like home, no matter how long you've been gone. In the summer of 2019, two of my former colleagues, Lisa Bowes, and Susy Tercini Antal, organized a TSN get-together.

People were there I hadn't seen in decades. We wore the years we'd earned, and not cheaply. Thanks to new streaming services and changes in government requirements for broadcasters, the industry was shrinking. A lot of people in the room had lost their jobs. Some were out of television completely. This could have been a bitter gathering. Instead, walking into that room was like stepping into a benevolent time machine. Connections resumed as if they'd ever been severed. Conversations flowed.

The biggest moment of the night was the arrival of Gordon Craig, the man who had risked everything on the belief that people would watch an all-sports channel. He'd made it work by hiring unproven, and inexpensive, talent. Remarkably, he let us do our jobs. We were thinly staffed so micromanaging probably wasn't an option anyway. Still, we were given our assignments and told to do them well.

When Gordon Craig walked in, everyone lined up to shake his hand and thank him for creating the workplace we all loved. He deflected the praise, instead thanking each person and giving the credit for the channel's success to us.

The evening reminded us that you can still belong someplace long after you've gone. It's not that you can go home again. It's that you never completely leave.

Somewhere along the line, I bought this TSN hat. It sports the new logo, inspired by TSNs partial ownership by ESPN, the American all-sports channel. I prefer the old logo, but this is still a solid cap.

Montreal Expos

Style: unstructured, snapback
Made by '47 Brand
Bought in Montreal in the summer of 2019

With Shane so vulnerable, our vacation options in the summer of 2019 were limited. We didn't want to get on an airplane, just in case Shane needed immediate medical attention. We couldn't go to a lake because we didn't want any water pressure on his brain. Shane wouldn't even let the shower hit that part of his head. If Shane wasn't swimming, neither were we. Also, there was no way we were leaving Canada's health-care umbrella. The family decided to go to Montreal and Ottawa.

The first stop was Montreal. A glorious walk around Mount Royal, a small mountain just west of downtown, wrecked my knees for the rest of the trip. The view of the skyline was well worth it though. Curtis, who loves big buildings, made sure we went up in Montreal's tallest building, 1000 de La Gauchetiere. We called it the Batman Building for its unique architecture.

We also visited Olympic Stadium, former home of the Expos. Montreal's CFL team, the Alouettes, were practicing outside. Curtis and I went up in the Big O's Tower section for another view of the city. I'd already acquired the only thing I wanted from the trip, this hat. The '47 Brand tri-color Expos hat was another option to my New Era 5950, which was getting old.

We usually did one or two things during the day, visiting a museum or seeing friends. Shane ordered poutine at almost every meal. His helmet was hot, and he liked to come back to the hotel, take off his hard plastic protection, and lay on his bed, playing games, or chatting with friends on his phone.

Our next stop was Ottawa, the capital of Canada. Shane got a kick out of the fact that the protestors in front of Parliament Hill needed to book their protests in advance. He even made up his own cause with its own chant.

"What do we want?"

"An end to procrastination!"

"When do we want it?"

"Tomorrow!"

While we were on the trip, we received a wonderful phone call. Shane's skull replacement surgery was scheduled for September third, nine months to the day after his first surgery. The call arrived just as we were sitting down to eat, so we ordered drinks and toasted the long-awaited news. Having an end date was a relief, but I wouldn't feel good again until the surgery was successfully completed.

Chicago Cubs
Style: structured, Velcro strapback
Made by New Era, 9forty
Gift from Diane Znamierowski Bassels

Diane Znamierowski Bassels is from Chicago and moved to Toronto when she married her husband, Chris. In 2016, I was the first person to hire her in Canada, an easy decision. Diane bursts with enthusiasm. She works hard and is loaded with talent, which means she had a lot in common with her colleagues at Love Nature. For three years, that team made a ton of good television with limited resources. The band was broken up in 2017 but they're still very close, which, as their former boss, makes me happy.

Diane played on my softball team for a year. In the summer of 2019, we worked together on a crime show. Diane and I agreed to a hat exchange. My favorite team is Detroit. Their hat has a D on the front, like Diane's first name. Her favorite team is the Cubs. Their hat has a C on the front, like my first name. So, I gave her a Tigers '47 Brand unstructured cap and she gave me this cool Cubs hat.

I love it. It's the only New Era 9forty hat I have. The Cubs hats look fantastic, with bright and hopeful colors and an understated C that doesn't try too hard. Mostly, I love that hat because it reminds me of my friendship with Diane, her husband, and the incredible crew at Love Nature. The best part of the job, by a wide margin, was working with them every day, watching them make wine from water.

I don't believe in having a work self and a home self. For some people, that's a necessary division to get the most work out of a staff. Productivity is important to me, but never more than the people providing it. I've been through too much death to see it any other way.

Clare Malcolm, a good friend who played sports with me and my high school friends, was killed in a car crash when she was twenty-five. While she was driving to a town outside Thunder Bay to teach school, a freak snowstorm caused her car to swerve into the path of a truck. My brother Scott, who dated her in high school, had to write the report for the newspaper. I'll never forget one of her students walking up the church aisle in his hockey jacket and laying a flower on her casket.

Danielle O'Gorman, the daughter of my great friend JohnO, was an avid and advanced horseback rider. One day she fell off her horse, then it stepped on her chest, crushing her heart, and killing her. She was just twelve.

Five of the fourteen people who played in our high school Blues Brothers band are dead.

Schoolmates of Shane and Curtis, Faris and Zain Abdille, thirteen and eight, were murdered by their father, who killed their mother as well, before he jumped off a bridge into oncoming traffic, ending his life, too. Shane was in Grade 5 and Curtis in Grade 1 when the tragedy happened. Faris, a few years older than Shane, had comforted him when he was being bullied in Grade 1. Shane spoke at the memorial service.

Ethan Vlachodimitris, one of Shane's closest friends, had died of a rare cancer just a week after his thirteenth birthday party. Shane was with him in the hospital hours before he passed.

And of course, Dave's death is with me always.

Our lives are precious. My coworkers aren't mere productivity machines. They're people with loves, losses, triumphs, and tragedies. Their lives matter more than anything they can do for a company, or a show, or for me. I tried to treat everyone that way always, especially the people who reported to me. Sticking up for my coworkers sometimes made me a pain to my bosses. There were times I'm sure it cost me professionally and I was more than OK with that tradeoff. Not that it mattered, but I never knew if my efforts were noticed. Not until Shane got sick.

When Shane was in the hospital, Gill Deacon, my partner in weightlessness from Discovery Channel, set up an online rotation to drop off food at our house. Gill did this a week before she started cancer treatment. The cooler outside our house was filled every night with meals provided for the most part by people I had worked with.

I didn't earn this kindness. The people who looked after us did it because they're outstanding, and I'm fortunate to know them. But I did something right somewhere. As Gill told me when she was admonishing me into accepting her offer (because I didn't want to inconvenience her during her cancer treatment), "Your people want to take care of you right now. You have to let them." My people came through for us, big time.

Pittsburgh Steelers
Style: structured, flexfit
Made by Reebok

We brought Shane to SickKids at 10:30 a.m., on September 3, 2019. The plastic surgeon, Dr. Forrest, talked to us after 11 p.m. He said he'd need two hours just for what he was doing, inserting a 3D-printed hard plastic skull section into the huge gap in Shane's skull and securing it.

After 2 p.m., Shane was brought into surgery. Nancy and I kissed our boy, then went to a waiting room filled with anxious parents. We watched a television screen on the wall to see when Shane went into the operating room and when he came out. His name wasn't listed, just a surgery number.

Hours passed. Doctors fresh from their operations greeted each parent, who left, relieved, one by one. At 6 p.m., Nancy and I were the only parents left in the room. We didn't talk much. Why was this taking so long? I couldn't indulge that thought. But it was also hard to keep it at bay.

Just after 6:30 p.m., Dr. Forrest walked in. Nancy and I bolted upright. He didn't keep us in suspense.

"I'm really happy with the surgery," he said. He said other things too but that was all I heard.

Shane was on his way to the intensive care unit. Nancy and I hugged, then let go of breaths we'd held for nine months. A nurse told us we could see Shane in just a few minutes.

When your child is sick, the worry is like water on rock, gradual but constant. Every bit of you is mustered to be strong and present for your children. You don't have the luxury of thinking about your own feelings.

Now that Shane was fixed, and we didn't have to worry about something falling on his exposed brain and doing permanent damage, I could let my own feelings out. I sat down in the corner, put my head in my hands, and sobbed.

A few minutes later, we walked into the ICU. Shane was groggy but protected. He could come home the next day. Nancy went back to the house to stay with Curtis, and I parked in a chair by Shane's bed. The nurse told me parents weren't allowed to be there overnight, but no one asked me to leave. The next day, Shane came home.

Five days later, the Steelers lost to the Patriots 33-3 on their way to an 8-8 season, terrible by Pittsburgh standards. It didn't bother me. Not anymore.

When I was younger sports were central to my existence, a place to belong when I didn't feel like I belonged anywhere. That hadn't been true for a long time. I belonged in my country, my industry, my friendships, and most importantly my family. Sports were in their proper place, a low-risk something-to-love, an enhancement, not an essential. The worst thing that could happen watching the Steelers was they could lose. Having lost friends and almost lost my son, dropping a game was refreshingly small potatoes. That's the way it should be. Besides, I was focused on a bigger contest.

Less than a month after surgery, Shane was back on the ice playing hockey again. Nancy was understandably worried as Shane took his first shift, coltish legs pushing his skates against the ice. I was thrilled. Tears filled my eyes all night. Shane was finally recovered.

The last word on this experience should go to Shane. Months earlier, while he was still wearing his helmet, Shane went out for lunch with me and a TSN friend, Doug Walton. Doug asked Shane how he dealt with his situation. Shane said, "I put up with the stuff I don't like and look forward to the things I do like. I spend as much time as I can doing things that make me happy. Just, be happy."

I bought this hat so I'd have a yellow Steelers cap to go with my black and white ones. I love this lid. The yellow pops and looks good with a black shirt. The shape is fantastic, and it feels great on my head. I didn't need another Steelers hat, but it made me happy, so I bought it anyway.

Brooklyn Dodgers
Style: structured, strapback
Made by '47 Brand

Things were looking good for me in February 2020. I was working on an episode of a train series for Exploration Production to air on Discovery Channel Canada. When that finished, they'd offered me a chance to direct a two-camera shoot on a luxury cruise from Argentina to Portugal, write the show, and take it through the edit suite.

Crooked Horse, the production company I worked for on "History in the Making," was talking to me about producing a pilot for a show for Discovery Channel US. Both were great options, and the future was rosy. By the end of March, both options were gone. Soon, both production companies were gone, too. In television, connections are everything, and the places where I'd established the most goodwill wouldn't be hiring again.

The start of the pandemic was gut-wrenching. I read an article that walked through the math on exponential growth. It showed how quickly COVID-19 could spread and overwhelm the supply of beds in our hospitals with sick patients. My heart started racing and my breath got short. I wondered if I had COVID-19. I soon recognized that I was just alarmed by what I was reading. I worried about my family getting sick, about running out of money, about everything.

Fortunately, the coping techniques we'd learned when Shane was sick helped my family. We had money in the bank and our expenses had dropped, so we lived in the moment and made the best of our days. At night we alternated watching movies and playing games. "You've Got Crabs," a card game Shane had picked up to play with his friends, was a favorite. Eventually, Shane wanted to spend some time online with his friends at night. Curtis, too. We eventually settled into a routine of ordering food and watching a TV series or movie on Friday nights.

At first, it seemed like we'd be locked down for a few months. I was guessing four, tops. While we were killing time, I decided to wear a different hat every day until people could gather again. I posted each hat on Facebook, with a line or two about what made it unique. Immediately, people started posting their own hats and telling their own stories. A community of hat lovers started connecting while we were isolated.

My Facebook friends needed this contact, and I did, too. Despite the coping mechanisms we'd developed during Shane's illness, the disappearance of work was a chest-tightening concern.

Fortunately, I have a philosophy I frequently put to work. There's what the world does to you, then there's what you do to yourself. Of course, it stings when bad things happen, but if we obsess over pain or injustice, we make it worse than it needs to be.

If you hold a dime right in front of your eye, it looks huge. That small coin can block out the world. If you hold it an arm's length from your face, that dime looks tiny. During the pandemic, I tried to push the problem back. There were days I would remind myself that I'm alive today. That my very existence is a small miracle of timing. I should just enjoy being here.

I also looked for ways to be productive. I created some videos on how to conduct interviews, to put something useful into the world. A teacher I know in Thunder Bay has been using them in her class.

To me, the pandemic will always be about testing our own resilience and trying to do the right thing. Both are reasons I love this Brooklyn Dodgers hat, which I bought for half price when I picked up my '47 Brand Tigers hat.

Jackie Robinson didn't break the color barrier because society evolved. He broke it because one man, Branch Rickey, decided it should be broken and another man, Jackie Robinson, had the ability and strength of character to show why it should fall. One did the right thing, the other had the resilience to see that it stuck. This hat felt right at home during hard times, especially as the demands for racial justice increased in the summer of 2020. If I hadn't been wearing a different hat every day, I would have worn this one almost all the time.

Texas Longhorns
Style: unstructured, strapback
Made by '47 Brand
Given to me by my cousin Julie

This was my first '47 Brand hat and the one that sparked my appreciation for unstructured caps. '47 Brand was started by Henry and Arthur D'Angelo, Italian immigrants who moved to Boston in 1938 when they were twelve. The brothers sold newspapers and memorabilia outside Fenway Park in Boston to make money. In 1947 they sold pennants celebrating the Red Sox 1946 American League Championship. That's the inspiration for the company name. It used to be called Twins Enterprises.

Eventually, the brothers expanded to hats and shirts, making enough money to buy property across the street from the stadium. Their storefront is a landmark in Boston. Arthur's four sons now run '47 Brand, which makes amazing hats for the four major pro sports and college teams. Family matters.

This hat was given to me by my cousin Julie.

Julie, who has excellent taste in hats, was one of the first people to share her own collection and was the first person to say I should turn the COVID-19 Hat Marathon into a book. Since she's a writer, I took the suggestion seriously. My mom, also a writer, seconded the notion.

And here we are.

Chicago White Sox

Style: structured, flexfit
Made by New Era, 39THIRTY
Given to me by Jim Nottingham

A few weeks after the COVID-19 hat marathon ended, a package arrived at the house. This hat was inside along with a lovely note. It was from Jim Nottingham, a retired Vietnam veteran from Texas. He and I had never met or spoken on a phone call or video conference. In the letter, he called me the Best Friend He's Ever Had that He Never Met.

Jim and I became Facebook friends by talking politics with a distant relative of mine and friend of his. When I started sharing hats, Jim immediately shared his. A lot of them were veterans' hats. He's said more than once that when he came home from the war, people turned on him. Our little group would share appreciation for Jim's hat of the day and thank him for his service. I'm not sure, but that may have been one reason he embraced the hat marathon with such enthusiasm. When Jim ran out of hats, he started sharing autographed pictures from blues legends, bobbleheads, and whatever he could get his hands on. He cleaned out his garage looking for treasures to share.

Jim was one of the first people to say he was sad the show-and-tell was over. He said the parade of lids helped him deal with the isolation we were all experiencing. I realized that this little project became a daily communion, coming together to experience parts of other people's lives. Some of my friends even became Jim's friends, commenting on his posts regularly.

Jason Simon, a friend and colleague, was a pitcher at Kansas State. I brought him in to show the coaches at East York House League how to teach pitching to the kids. He told us that once the pitch leaves your hand, you don't control it anymore. That's true for creative endeavors, too. You put yourself into something then send it into the world. Once it has been released, you don't know what's going to happen.

I am happy to see my COVID-19 hat marathon went out into the world and created friendships. I'm also grateful for Jim, and this excellent hat.

Dome Productions
Style: structured, strapback
Given to me by Dome Productions in 2019

For all the pandemic had taken away, it had also given us the gift of time. I knew I had to make the most of it. After the television work disappeared, I started marketing my company, colbyvision, to businesses, as well as production companies and broadcasters. Since I wanted people to identify me with storytelling and helping businesspeople, I started two online video podcasts, "Narrative Drivetime," where I interviewed storytellers and "the Business Heroes," where I interviewed business owners about their journeys. I had no idea if this attempt at marketing would work.

It did. Bob Baker, who was a year ahead of me in the Communications Studies program at the University of Windsor, sent me a note. He'd seen my posts and knew about colbyvision. Bob now worked at the Aga Khan Museum in Toronto. The institution celebrates Muslim history and culture.

Their fall fundraiser couldn't be held in person, so they wanted to create an online event. It couldn't look like a big Zoom call, Bob said. He wanted it to feel more like watching CNN.

"Is this something colbyvision does?'

"Yes," I told him.

Now, I hadn't produced a project like this through my company yet, but I'd made plenty of shows like this throughout my career. Bob sent me the treatment for the event, and I turned in a request for proposal, competing against two other bidders. The museum wanted panel discussions about the big issues of the day and some artist performances. They also wanted some live elements. I called my friends down at Dome Productions, the production studio inside the Rogers Centre, where the Toronto Blue Jays play. I told them my plan and asked for a quote.

I can't remember ever wanting anything so badly. This was a chance to do a high-profile production through my own company, a show I designed, budgeted, pitched, and won myself. It was step one to really being my own business.

I won the bid.

For the next seven weeks, I worked with artists, musicians, hosts, a comedian, some great thinkers, and the wonderful staff at the Aga Khan Museum. People were dedicated, talented, and kind. They also valued my expertise.

During the last two days of the project, I worked in a control room at Dome Productions. The first day we recorded the panels and assembled parts of the show. The last day was the big one, when we recorded host links, put the show together, then streamed it on YouTube. There would be two live hits in the show, including the ending.

I prepared my material as thoroughly as I could, trying to anticipate any eventuality, then had one drink, to help me sleep, and was in bed by eleven, fortifying myself with a full eight hours of sleep.

That night, I dreamed I was playing football. I was the left defensive end, and the coach was screaming at me. "Why aren't you getting to the quarterback? GET THE QUARTERBACK!" I was determined to take down that hotshot on the other side of the line of scrimmage. I set myself in a four-point stance, both hands and feet on the ground, the muscles in my legs coiled, ready to explode as soon as the ball was snapped. I stared at the ball, unblinking. The moment the ball moved, I launched. BANG! A huge collision rocked my body.

I immediately, sat up in bed. A river of blood poured down my forehead across the right side of my face. I had smacked headfirst into my night table. The sound woke up Nancy. I rushed to the bathroom for a towel. Blood dripped on the floor as I walked down the hall. I mopped the red mess off my face and looked at the wound. It was about the length of my pinkie fingernail. A stitch would probably be a good idea. Nancy brought me a towel filled with ice and I sat on the couch in the living room.

It was 4 a.m. I had to be at Dome Production at two in the afternoon. I took out my phone and checked for concussion symptoms. I had none, but it was still early. Going to sleep was a bad idea. Going to the hospital, even if I needed a stitch, was out of the question because I could be in there for hours. Also, the hospitals were filled with COVID-19 patients. So, I waited it out on the couch, hoping the wound would close enough to keep me from bleeding all over myself in front of the crew and my client. The cut was just under the hair line and blood shows up well on gray hair like mine.

By early afternoon, the cut was seeping a little bit, but occasional dabs with a tissue would take care of that. There was a small bump under the hairline around the cut. Otherwise, my head felt fine. Nancy wanted to be extra cautious, so she drove me to Rogers Centre and would pick me up afterward. This was an abundance of caution.

In the control room, we taped links with the host, standup comedian and CBC presenter Ali Hassan, who was at the museum. Then we packaged the show. I was buzzing with excitement. I was back in a control room, overseeing a production I had created. Larry was watching on YouTube at home and texting me feedback throughout the show. What a good friend.

We went live twice during the show. No big problems. At the end of the night, after the event had raised $840,000 for the museum, I watched my animated logo roll at the end of the credits.

That was my highlight of the night.

The next day, I sent out thank-you notes to all involved.

I was as proud of this two-hour show, assembled in less than two months, than I was of anything I had ever done. The content was about social issues that were important to me, and the arts, which I love. I developed the show with an old university classmate and some new friends. It ran through Dome Productions, overseen by Mary Ellen Carlyle, another University of Windsor grad who had brought my resume into TSN back in 1988. She got me into the business. I was starting to feel good about this new chapter in my career.

As for my late-night collision, I texted the story to my brothers. They thought it was hilarious. I told them I was taken out by a pulling night table. Jim asked, "Did you move the table?"

"Not much. It was up against the wall."

The worst part of it all? In the dream, I was only in a practice. I bashed my head for a dream practice! Wrecking myself for a dream game would have been OK.

Dome Productions gave me this sweet hat. It's light, perfect for the summer, and exquisitely shaped. The silver stitching on the gray hat with an understated teal accent is subtle and beautiful. This cap reminds me of a win when I really needed one.

Pittsburgh Steelers
Style: structured, flexfit
Made by New Era. 39THIRTY

There are two reasons I have so many hats. This Pittsburgh Steelers hat, my most recently purchased, represents one of them. I already had structured hats in black, white, and yellow, two Super Bowl Champions hats, and two unstructured hats from '47 Brand. All the category boxes had been ticked. Then this hat came along with a contrasting yellow brim, a charcoal cap, and the Steelers sleeve stripe on one side. Asymmetric design has a little swagger. The low-rise dome looks good on my head, too. I certainly didn't need another cap, but this one enticed me.

When New Era started selling official Major League Baseball hats in the back of "The Sporting News" in 1978, they elevated baseball hats for the everyday consumer. Design and structure became part of the package. Thanks to New Era's influence, I learned to appreciate other great cap makers, like '47 Brand, Fanatics, and Zephyr. Sometimes, I go online and look at hats, just to appreciate them.

Here's the takeaway for people who love a hat fan: no matter how many hats they have, you can still buy them one. Before you do, though, ask about their favorites, likes and dislikes, then buy them a high-quality product. Cap lovers know the difference between a bad hat and a great one.

Detroit Tigers—Home
Style: structured, fitted
Made by New Era, 5950

My favorite hat is the Detroit Tigers New Era 5950 home cap. The asymmetrical old English D is classy, timeless. The gleaming white D on a midnight canvas is a classic in contrast. Everyone looks good in this cap. I think this is my second New Era 5950 Tigers home cap. The olde English D stitching isn't raised and the MLB logo isn't on the back, so I must have bought it before 1992.

This lid represents the second reason I have so many hats. I still have this cap, even though I have four newer versions, because what it lacks in structure it makes up for in memories. I wore this hat in Tiger Stadium, sitting next to Dave, scooping infield dirt off the rolled-up tarp. I didn't understand the power of the memories in each hat until I started wearing every one of them in 2020. Every day, I was transported, even in lockdown. I experienced New York City with my mom and dad, or Wrigley Field with my closest friends. I was falling in love or coaching my sons. I was also at a funeral or in a hospital.

For me, the hats aren't just shaped cloth. They're connections to the people I love and the best moments in my life. Wearing my life helped me appreciate it more. I hope that reading this book has inspired you to do the same.

Life will lift you up, then punch you in the face. Whatever brings you joy—Beanie Babies, Birkenstocks, or Barry Manilow—go all in, unapologetically. Hold onto all the happiness you can.

Acknowledgements

This book never would have happened if a core group of hat lovers hadn't decided to share the caps and stories. Thanks to Ken Barhu, Sandy Slater Barnaby, Jeff Blundell, Julie Candoli, Bill King, Alix MacDonald, Tevis Marcum, Zach Monash, Jim Nottingham, Kevin Rzepa, Chuck Steele, and Marc Stevens for turning communication into community.

Participation wouldn't have turned into pages without my cousin Julie's suggestion and my mother Dorothy Colby and brother Scott Colby's agreement. All three are excellent writers, so I listened to their recommendations. Julie Hewett's The One Thing reading group and follow-up "66 Days to a Habit" challenge showed me how to carve out time to write the book. Thanks to all of you for making this happen.

Seven beta readers agreed to look at my early draft and give me feedback. My brother Scott had great ideas and my wife Nancy Adderley-Colby contributed outstanding copy editing. Joey Buchholz and Ryan Folwell provided a sports fan's perspective. Seonaid Eggett's insight shaped the structure of each chapter. Marc Stevens and Catherine Annau added much-needed big-picture comments. Thank you so much for your insight.

Mark Foerster, an outstanding cameraman and good friend, took the cover photo. Vika Kachcovska treated all the pictures, which were shot at my desk under bad lighting—because I didn't think this would ever become a book. Vika also designed the hot logo for radX, which appears on a hat in the book. Pellegrino Castronovo suggested creating the videos, which you can access through the QR codes in the book. Thanks to all of you.

Laura Boast was the last person to review the book. She provided outstanding copy editing and pushed me to dig deeper. Some of the best segments in the book are the result of her enthusiastic prompting. Thank you so much.

This book could not have been published without a whole lot of permissions. The rights to use the hats were given by Katie Steiner at Major League Baseball, Carrie Adams at Minor League Baseball, Aries Tabigue at the National Football League, Michael Potenza at the National Basketball Association, Alison Nunez at the National Hockey League, Bryan Ramsden at the Canadian Football League, Lindsay Victor of Learfield IMG College for permission to use the University of Michigan and University of Texas hats, Mary-Ellen Carlyle at Dome Productions, Valeria Foncea Rubens at the Atacama, Large Millimeter/Submillimeter Array, Michael Clarke at the East York Baseball Association, Dave Tommasini at Four Seasons Aviation, Donna Kaufman at NatureFootage, Julia Padfield at Shakespeare's Globe, Matt "Marshall" Hoemann from Bluecentric, Anna Buckley and Martin Lajoie of Parks Canada, Bryan Graham of the Thunder Bay Border Cats, Greg Balec for the Thunder Bay Whiskey Jacks, Jessica Fergesen from the Cedar Rapids Kernels, Don Lewis of the Auburn Doubledays, Andre Lachance of Baseball Canada, Jon Arklay of Bell Media, Astrid Zimmer of Blue Ant Media, Matthias Beier of Shoei, David Mack and Kate Rahn of Peterbilt, Rick Baetz and Tricia Lyle of the New Era Cap Company, Max Christiansen of Mint Green Group on behalf of '47 Brand, Zeke Gendill of Zephyr Hats, Egan Malley and Burke Kronenberger at American Needle, and Curtis Begg of Puma.

Some very personal permissions were granted, too. Thanks to Darcy Hagberg, Valerie Hagberg, Ryan Hagberg, Ben Hagberg, and Relita Misa for signing off on the book. Thanks also to my wife, Nancy and my sons, Shane and Curtis for allowing me to share parts of their lives. The same is true for Peter Colby, Dorothy Colby, Jim Colby, Scott Colby, Lynn Southcott, Danielle Colby, Mitch Colby, Natasha Mistry, Isaac Colby, and Savanne Colby. Thanks to you all for your generosity.

A heartfelt thank you goes out to the makers of quality hats. When I was young, caps were terrible. They seemed to be created as an afterthought. Now, they are masterpieces. A special shout-out to the New Era Cap company, the first organization to grant permission and believe in this project, '47 Brand and Fanatics. You all do great work.

Thanks to the University of Windsor for teaching me to write, and to my mentors at TSN, and Discovery Channel who helped me refine my skills.

Finally, thanks to all whose love and kinship put meaning into my hats, especially Dave Hagberg, whose friendship still shapes my life. It's not about the headwear, it's the life lived in it.

I tip my cap to you all.

Craig Colby

Not all my hats made it into the book. To see the other hats and read their stories, scan this code with the camera on your phone.

For more content from Craig, including his blog and some podcasts, visit www.colbyvision.net.

CPSIA information can be obtained
at www.ICGtesting.com
Printed in the USA
BVHW090857240622
640261BV00003B/3